George A Potter

The Instrument of Association

A Manual of Currency

George A Potter

The Instrument of Association
A Manual of Currency

ISBN/EAN: 9783744753784

Printed in Europe, USA, Canada, Australia, Japan

Cover: Foto ©Andreas Hilbeck / pixelio.de

More available books at **www.hansebooks.com**

THE

INSTRUMENT OF ASSOCIATION.

A

MANUAL OF CURRENCY.

BY

GEORGE A. POTTER.

Political economy, at least, is found to have sound principles, founded in the moral and physical nature of man, which, however lost sight of in particular measures, — however even temporarily controverted and borne down by clamor, — have yet a stronger and stronger testimony borne to them in each succeeding generation, by which they must, sooner or later, prevail. — HERSCHEL.

In all countries, however, men seem at last to have been determined by irresistible reasons to give the preference, for this employment, to metals above every other commodity. — *Origin and Use of Money.* — ADAM SMITH.

NEW YORK:

PUBLISHED BY HURD AND HOUGHTON.

Cambridge: Riverside Press.

1868

CONTENTS.

INTRODUCTION.

THE author of this book has been impelled, by a sense of the deplorable and almost universal ignorance of the true theory of money, which prevails among all classes of the community, — in Congress, in the Treasury Department of the government, in the various Chambers of Commerce throughout the country, and among the members of the press, — to demonstrate as briefly as possible, not his own opinion upon the subject, but the LAW, as laid down by the most eminent writers on political economy, and as confirmed again and again by the history of modern nations. The consequences of this ignorance to our own country have been most ruinous, immeasurably evil, and well-nigh irremediable. The fiscal administration of the government since the close of the war, has been characterized by the most fatal ignorance and disregard of the laws of political economy, while the people are being rapidly impoverished, and sunk deeper and deeper (government and people alike) into the bottomless abyss of bankruptcy. And yet, while many are sensible of this disastrous tendency, both the legislative and executive departments of the government seem to be utterly imbecile, and wholly incapable of agreeing upon any salutary measure of reform. Indeed, the whole cause of this unfortunate condition of affairs, seems to be entirely obscured from the vision of those whose high duty it is to provide for the general welfare of the country. The press, in the mean time, teems with chimeras of every conceivable shape, and pamphlets are multiplied upon pamphlets, till universal bewilderment seems to have settled, like a dense fog, upon and around the whole subject. The country is in a position similar to that at the close of the Revolution, and on the whole, perhaps, a worse condition than then. Since then, it has never been in a situation approaching that in which it now is. The evils of paper money — a revolutionary currency — are upon us, and the common fate of nations under the devastating influences of such a currency can only be averted by a careful consideration and observance of the laws of political economy. It has been the aim of the author to elucidate, as clearly as possible, the laws which

regulate the value of money, and to show how
these natural, immutable laws have been violated;
and also, to show that it is owing to this auda-
cious, reprehensible defiance and violation of these
eternal laws, that such overshadowing calamities
are threatening the destruction of public and
private credit. The author has not attempted
to propound any new doctrine. There is no
new doctrine. The law as laid down by Adam
Smith and affirmed by John Adams nearly a
century ago, is still the same, — yesterday, to-
day, and forever. The law is substantially this:
that the value of the currency of a nation is
limited by natural law; that whenever this limit
is exceeded, whether the currency be of coin or
paper, it becomes depreciated; that if the depreciated currency be of coin, the precious metals
will be exported, till the volume of the currency
is brought within the limit; that if the depreciated currency be of paper, it must remain depreciated, and if it be considerably depreciated,
it can never be disposed of except at its depreciated value, — that is to say, it cannot be restored
to the true standard, by contraction or funding;
that if a paper currency be issued *ad infinitum*,
the whole value of the issue can never exceed the
natural limit. To state this law specifically, it

will be sufficient to say, that if the natural limit of the currency be $500,000,000, and the nominal paper issues be $1,500,000,000, the paper dollars are not worth more than thirty-three and one third cents each. If the natural limit be $500,000,000, and it were possible to put $1,500,000,000 coin in use as currency, then the value of these dollars would only be equal to one third the value of the dollars that were in use previous to the increase; that is to say, the price of all commodities would be three times as great. *Price* and *value* are quite distinct from each other. Price is the power to command money. Value is the power to command labor. The author has been enabled to ascertain the natural limit of the currency of this country, and to fix its true value, beyond controversy. He has also been enabled to arrive at the approximate nominal value of the irredeemable paper currency, and has demonstrated, incontestably, that the present value of our legal tender and national bank-notes is about thirty-three and one third cents each in the common currency of the world. He has shown that the fiscal embarrassments of the nation, as well as the almost frightful amount of our foreign indebtedness, are wholly due to the dogged persistence of the

Treasury Department, in maintaining the price of the legal tender notes above seventy cents, when their value is only about thirty-three and one third cents — in selling gold and tampering with the currency. Congress is obnoxious to censure in the highest degree, for conferring such corrupt and corrupting power upon the Minister of Finance, though he be the most pure and incorruptible of men. If pure-minded, he is almost as ignorant as Congress, and has wielded a terribly destructive power, without hindrance, and with the most disastrous results. Congress, in this respect, it cannot be denied, has manifested utter incapacity for good, and capacity only for evil. The Administration is, perhaps, equally to blame; for the Finance Minister should, by virtue of his office, be able to inform Congress upon the true principles of political economy. But, unfortunately, fitness for office seems to work a disqualification therefor, in this country. Not only has this fatal policy of selling gold been persisted in, but the equally fatal dogma of contraction has been pursued with a relentlessness of purpose which deserves the execrations of every citizen. History furnishes no instance where an irredeemable paper currency, — revolutionary currency, or bills of credit, — when once issued to great excess, has ever been considerably appreciated in value ; and history never will furnish such an instance, for the simple reason that it is impossible. The very attempt to do so necessitates increased issues, because it destroys the revenues of the government.

The attempt has been pursued with greater obstinacy and to a greater extent, perhaps, in this country than ever before. The currency cannot be contracted, still less can it be funded. The only method of disposing of this currency is such as has been employed by other nations, and which is pointed out in the text. The maladministration of the Treasury Department has been the greatest tax upon the people, but there are others equally unjust. The national bank circulation is a tax upon the people to the extent of about fifteen millions of dollars per annum, and, unfortunately, the system, while ostensibly under the control of Congress, has or seems to have its attorneys in both legislative branches, and in the various departments of the Treasury. It is not fit that the people should be compelled to bear this incubus longer. The dominant party seems to be without the moral courage to resist it, if, indeed, the party itself be not within its stern control. An enormous income tax, without color of legality under the fundamental law, endurable during the war, but intolerable now that the war is ended, has pressed heavily upon the middling classes, and in many cases encroached upon their capital. The excise on distilled spirits, one of the most just and least oppressive of taxes, seems to be appropriated by the vultures who hover about and pollute all departments of the government, and sit at the receipt of customs. Preposterous imposts have been levied upon foreign products, with the futile design of shutting them out from ruinous competition with home industry ; but the money king, whom Congress has enthroned above the law, and the smuggler, laugh them to scorn. It is not easy to contemplate these things with composure, nor is it agreeable to dwell upon the criminal neglect of the interests of the country, when one's political sympathies are drawn towards the dominant party. But the country has stronger and paramount claims, even if each person's individual interest did not constrain him to rebuke those, who, intoxicated with power, apparently care for little else than its retention. It is true that a factious opposition has been presented to the legislative power, but it cannot be concealed that the dominant party has retained a controlling power of the machinery of legislation, and, instead of a well-devised system of taxation, we seem to have an artful scheme of spoliation. The author has discussed the question of subjecting the capital invested in government bonds to taxation with entire freedom, as he was in duty bound to do. Whoever has read history attentively, will perceive the danger likely to arrive from this exemption of accumulated property of any description from taxation, and throwing the burden upon production. The history of the French Revolution is most instructive in this particular. It was the refusal of the nobles and privileged classes in France to submit to taxation, and to acquiesce in the wholesome reforms proposed by Turgot, and afterwards by Necker, which drove the latter repeatedly from office, necessitated the issue of paper money, brought on the Reign of Terror, and culminated in the ascendancy of the military power. The frightful sequence of events in France could not have taken place, had the suffrage been general and impartial, and therefore, such calamities are impossible here. The danger is not that injustice will be done to the tax-payers in this country, but that the at-

tempt to commit a wrong upon them, either in
exempting bonds from taxation or in settling the
public debt by a standard thrice as high as that
by which it was contracted, will react with fatal
injustice to the public creditor, and be prejudicial
in the last degree to the permanence of the
Union. Especially has it been the desire of the
author to embody the elementary principles of
currency in the smallest possible compass, since
it is well-nigh impossible to induce the general
community to undertake the careful perusal of
an elaborate treatise on political economy. He
has drawn freely from the fountains of knowledge
and the history of human experience. He has
commented with freedom upon the executive and
legislative departments of the government, as
well as upon the political party which is in the
ascendant, and he conceives it was his right and
duty so to do. He has done this with none
other than kind feelings, so far as any persons in
either department of the government are known
to him. He has not sought popularity at the
expense of truth, but rather incurred the risk of
censure for the sake of justice. He has en-
deavored to submit to the guidance of his in-
stincts, which, he hopes, are patriotic, honest, and
republican. So far as he may have advanced

principles of political economy, he invites intelligent criticism. So far as he may be judged in matters of opinion, or in the manner of this book, he invokes fairness only.

GEO. A. POTTER.

BROOKLYN, *June* 4, 1868.

INSTRUMENT OF ASSOCIATION.

—◆—

I.

ITS NATURE AND USE IN THE ECONOMY OF SOCIETY.

THE credit of a state depends on the proportion of its revenue to its expense, and the ease and satisfaction with which the necessary taxation is borne by the people.[1] The revenue of a state depends entirely upon the industry of the people, for labor is the only source of wealth. The industry of the people consists in utilizing the matter already created by God. Man produces nothing but utility.[2] The industry of man takes three general but different forms — transmutation, transformation, transportation.[3] TRANSMUTATION is the appropriation and change of matter by the agriculturist, miner, chemist, hunter, fisherman, and so on. TRANSFORMATION is the change of form wrought by the manufacturer, which branch of human industry is susceptible of the greatest extension of the prin-

[1] Burke.　　[2] McCulloch and Mill.　　[3] Walker.

ciple of the division of labor.[1] The greater the
extent of the division of labor, the greater its
efficiency in the aggregate; hence, manufacturing industry is the most profitable for any nation, so long as it can obtain a market for its
products at home or abroad. TRANSPORTATION
is the change of place wrought by the merchant,
the seaman, and the carrying and distributing
trade generally; in a word, it is commerce.
This branch of industry is also susceptible, in
a great degree, of the application of the principle of the division of labor, and includes bankers,
brokers, and dealers in money generally, so far
as they help to utilize capital. These are the producing classes, and so far as the value of their
production exceeds the value of their consumption, so far have they increased the fixed or circulating capital of the country. The prosperity
of each class is intimately associated with, and
dependent on, the prosperity of the other two.
If from any cause the prosperity of manufacturing industry declines, agriculture and commerce will also decline.[2] The one grand con-
necting link between these three general branches
of industry, in all their multifarious subdivisions,

---

[1] *Progress of the Mechanical Arts. A Lecture before the
Boston Mechanics' Institution.* 1828. Webster.

[2] Webster.

— the one *instrument of association*,[1]— is money and its substitutes, comprehended in the general term — currency.

It is obvious that the material welfare of a state depends upon the perfect adaptability of the instrument of association. And in order to be perfectly adapted to its functions, it must promote a rapid *societary circulation*.[2] By a rapid societary circulation, is meant rapid production, and interchange, and consumption, of the products of labor. The more rapid the circulation, the more perfect the power of association, the greater the power to support taxation, the greater the economy of labor, the more advanced the civilization of the community, the greater the extent of the division of labor, and the more secure the democratic form of government and the liberty of the people.[3] The instrument of association then must not be unwieldy, otherwise the circulation will be sluggish ; if the currency is excessive, it begins to lose the character of a medium and becomes itself the thing to be

1 I am indebted to Mr. Carey for this term. No other language so completely embodies the idea developed in this book as to the functions of the currency. Hence the appropriateness of the title.

2 Carey.

3 De Tocqueville. "Industry is essentially social." — *Everett.*

circulated.   It must be elastic, otherwise values
and prices will be constantly fluctuating ; producers will stop producing and begin speculat-
ing, and the demoralization and poverty of the
people will ensue.   It must possess the element of
value in itself, or by proxy, in order to command
value at all times.   It must be as inexpensive
as possible, otherwise it will be a burden on the
people.   Finally, it must be self-regulating and
secured against the interference of empirics,
whether in the executive or legislative departments of the government.[1]   In order to illus-
trate, by analogy, the economy of a rapid circulation, let us suppose a given quantity of freight
to be transported from one point to another.
This freight, we will suppose, can be transported
by one hundred cars making one trip per day,
or it can be transported by ten cars making ten
trips per day.   Now it is obvious that when the
ten cars only are employed as the instrument of
commerce, the more rapid will be the circulation,
and the less expensive in point of cost will be
that instrument of commerce.   Let us also suppose that the use of a thousand cars every day
to transport this freight is made compulsory ;

[1] " He who tampers with the currency, robs labor of its
bread." — *Webster.*

then, obviously, the instrument of commerce is not only very expensive, but each car will only be a tenth part loaded. In these supposed cases the utility of the ten cars, and the hundred cars, and the thousand cars is the same. Their respective values as instruments of commerce are equal. So it is with the currency of a nation; the momentum [1] (mass multiplied by velocity), or utility, being the same when the volume of the currency is small and the circulation rapid, as when the volume is large and the circulation sluggish.[2] Hence, the smaller the volume of the currency of a nation, the more rapid the circulation, and the greater the material prosperity of such nation.[3] The *minimum* as well as the *maximum* of the volume of the currency of a nation, however, is fixed by a principle which will be laid down hereafter. The elasticity of the currency of a nation depends upon its material, and whether there be any use for such material within or without such nation, other than for currency. If the currency be of irredeemable paper, it will have no elasticity, because its

---

[1] Bowen and Perry.   [2] Mill.

[3] Mr. Carey contradicts this proposition, but Smith, Hume, and nearly all the British economists, as well as Say, Bastiat, and Chevalier, sustain it. Bowen, Walker, and Perry also substantially admit it.

volume remaining the same, the constant ebbing
and flowing of the tide of commerce will fall as
upon the sea-shore, marking a depreciation, or
it will rise as upon the sea-shore, marking an
appreciation of the currency. If the currency
be of inherent or representative value, it will go
abroad or be consumed when in excess; when
deficient, it will be increased by accretions from
abroad, or by production. 'The ceaseless opera-
tion of the eternal law of supply and demand,
which acts on everything of value, whether
movable or immovable, will cause a currency of
value to remain, or go where it will command
the greatest value of other commodities in exchange.' It is rather a truism than a similitude
to say that the laws of trade will preserve a perfect adjustment of a currency of value, just as
the law of gravitation preserves a perfect level
of the sea. In saying that the currency must
possess the element of value in itself, it is intended to use the word value in the sense given
to it by Bastiat; that is to say, it must be the
embodiment of human service or labor already
performed, or rather it must embody the power
to command service or labor. It doubtless seems
paradoxical to assert that a metallic currency is
comparatively inexpensive, but experience has

proved it to be the cheapest currency that human
ingenuity can devise. Its utmost cost is the loss
of interest, and the insignificant loss by abra-
sion. It is the cheapest because it is the most
efficient ; [1] but if we consider the immense loss
resulting to private individuals and corporations, and to the industrial classes and capital-
ists, from the frequent expansions and revul-
sions of a paper currency, the absurdity of the
pretense that such a currency is cheap, will
be readily perceived. The Secretary of the
Treasury, in 1841, in answer to a request of
Congress, estimated that up to that time the
losses sustained by the government and the people by allowing banks of issue, was $380,943,-
497. [2]

Having described the essentials of a perfect
currency or instrument of association, it only remains to say that of all materials known to
civilized man, the precious metals alone possess
all the indispensable qualities of a perfect currency. It is the opinion of many able writers,
that the precious metals were designed by the
Creator to be the instrument of association. It
is no figure of speech to say (and I speak it
with the utmost reverence), in the language of a

[1] Walker.   [2] Ibid.

stump-orator, that gold and silver is the money
of God and of democracy.[1] The pernicious
doctrine of Adam Smith, that paper could be
advantageously substituted for a metallic circulation, thus displacing the coin with an instrument
less costly, has been abundantly refuted by experience, and it may well be doubted whether he
would not be an implacable enemy of paper
money in any form, were he now living. It
should be borne in mind that when Smith wrote,
the science of political economy was in its in-
fancy; indeed, he has been regarded as its fa-
ther; moreover, political economy is an experimental science; it assumes nothing but the
universality of human selfishness, which is a
law of human nature.[2] But if history has
proved anything, it has proved that a paper
currency intended to be convertible at all times,
under any circumstances, into gold at the will
of the holder, is a chimera, and nowhere more
so, than under a popular government. Political
economy, therefore, being an experimental science, it must be conceded that on the facts as
they are in history, a paper currency cannot
stand the test to which that science subjects
all theories, before admitting them to be sound.

---

[1] Speech of S. S. Cox.   [2] Bowen.

Adam Smith, however, entertained a wholesome contempt for circulating notes of small denomination, for he says, " Where the issuing of bank-notes for such very small sums is allowed, and commonly practiced, many mean people are both enabled and encouraged to become bankers. A person whose promissory note for five pounds, or even twenty shillings, would be rejected by everybody, will get it to be received without scruple when it is issued for so small a sum as a sixpence. But the frequent bankruptcies to which such beggarly bankers must be liable, may occasion a very considerable inconveniency, and sometimes a very great calamity to many poor people who had received their notes in payment. It were better, perhaps, that no bank-notes were issued in any part of the kingdom for a smaller sum than five pounds." Speaking of the lawfulness of restricting the issue of circulating notes, Dr. Smith further says : " Such regulations may no doubt be considered as in some respects a violation of natural liberty. But those exertions of the natural liberty of a few individuals, which might endanger the whole society, are, and ought to be, restrained by the laws of all governments ; of the most free, as well as the most despotical. The

obligation of building party walls, in order to
prevent the communication of fire, is a violation
of natural liberty, exactly of the same kind with
the regulations of the banking trade which are
here proposed." The arguments of those who
advocate paper money, do not differ widely from
those of John Law, who held " that money owes
its value to the public confidence ; and that paper, or anything else, may answer this purpose
as well as the precious metals (the first, as well
as the last, he regarded as the mere signs of
wealth); that land was a better commodity for
money than silver, and that the currency of a
country might be increased to the whole value
of its lands; that the effect of such an increase
would be not depreciation, but merely a lower-
ing of interest, by which trade would be
encouraged and wealth augmented." [1] Notwithstanding that such a fallacious doctrine has been
again and again exploded, it seems to find new
advocates in every generation. These advocates
do not, perhaps, claim that land is a suitable
basis for a circulation, but they do claim that
interest-bearing bonds are a safe basis for circulation, which is equally a heresy. Government
bonds are not money, and as a basis of circula-

[1] *The Mississippi Scheme in France.* — Tucker.

tion, " the mischief is, that they are least available when they are most wanted; the very causes which might prevent the banks from redeeming their issues promptly, would cause a fall in the value of the stocks and mortgages on the ultimate security of which their notes have been issued." [1]   A circulation based on government bonds is a circulation based on debt, and not on value, than which, nothing can be conceived more unsubstantial.   A circulation based on staple merchandise of general consumption throughout the world, and imperishable in its own nature, such as cotton, valued at about the cost of production in the chief producing country, and rendered secure against damage by fire and water, would be a comparatively sound currency, but much more expensive than a circulation based on gold.   With such a currency, the element of value would be ever present; but it is precisely this evasion of value and the substitution of debt in its place, which is always sought; this foisting upon the people as money that which, when put to the crucial test, has always been found to be its counterfeit and not its representative, which is always persisted in ; it is this insufferable fraud on the people, originally

1 Gouge, quoted by Bowen.

granted as a privilege, but now claimed as a right, which has been the abundant cause of so much loss and distress in the mercantile community, so much discord between capital and labor, such acrimonious strife between free-traders and protectionists, and the remote cause of civil war in the country. If the instrument of association be imperfect, the power of association becomes weakened, and the danger of dissociation is always impending. Men are too apt to regard this Union as the result of extraordinary abnegation on the part of our fathers, with a view to demonstrate, in the uncontaminated society of a new world, a liberal principle of political philosophy which had hitherto failed elsewhere. That the framers of the Constitution, especially Washington who presided at the convention, were animated by such lofty sentiments, is not doubted; but that the States and people at large participated in, and were influenced by patriotic considerations to any important degree, neither history nor a knowledge of the springs of human action will permit us to believe. The recorded failure of the Confederation to promote the general prosperity, was regarded as a proof of what the exigencies of the Union demanded in a general government.[1]

[1] *History of the Constitution*, Curtis.

That the evils of paper money were generally considered to be the parent of the commercial distress, is perfectly clear. "One of the principal causes which led to the experiment of making a national government with power to prevent such abuses, had been the frauds and injustice perpetrated by the States, in their issues of paper money; and there was at this very time a loud and general outcry against the conduct of the people of Rhode Island, who had kept themselves aloof from the national convention, for the express purpose, among others, of retaining to themselves the power to issue such a currency."[1]   But the exigencies of the Union demanded that no State should "make anything but gold and silver coin a tender in payment of debts,"[2] and so the prohibition was incorporated into the fundamental law.[3] "Whatever we may think of it now, the Constitution had its immediate origin in the conviction of the necessity for this uniformity or identity in commercial regulations. The whole history of the country, of every year and every month, from the close of the war of the Revolution to 1789, proves this. Over whatever other interests it was made

---

[1] *History of the Constitution*, Curtis.   [2] Ibid.
[3] *Constitution*, art. 1, sec. 10.

to extend, and whatever other blessings it now
confers, or hereafter may confer, on the millions
of free citizens who do or shall live under its
protection ; even though in time to come, it shall
raise a pyramid of power and grandeur, whose
apex should look down on the loftiest political
structures of other nations and other ages, it will
yet be true, that it was itself the child of press-
ing commercial necessity."[1]   It is readily conceded that slavery was the immediate cause of
the late civil war, but slavery grew and flourished
under a condition of society that was wholly due
to the inefficacy of the instrument of association.
This will be shown hereafter.[2]

[1] Webster.   [2] *Post*, pp. 101-104.

II.

OF ITS COMPONENT PARTS.

THE circulating medium of a country, whether of notes or coin, is commonly supposed to form the entire currency thereof, whereas, only a very small portion of the commercial exchanges is effected by circulating notes or coin. The greater portion of our commercial exchanges are effected by bank deposits, represented and transferred by means of checks. The magnitude of the exchanges effected at the clearing house in New York, without the intervention of circulating notes, is very great. The larger proportion of customs duties are paid by coin certificates of deposit, and before the use of these, certified gold checks were the common means of effecting exchanges in a gold currency. The mercantile classes seldom use circulating notes in payments of one hundred dollars or more. In the seventeenth century, the commercial currency of some of the smaller European states consisted entirely of deposits.[1] The banks of Venice, Genoa, Amster-

1 Smith.

dam, Hamburg, and Nuremburg, held deposits of bullion, which was considered the standard money, and was transferred by means of receipts which were in the nature of certificates of deposit. This practice arose in consequence of the coin of those states having become degraded by clipping, and by the admixture of foreign coin in the circulation, so that bank money commonly bore an agio ; that of the Bank of Hamburg was about fourteen per cent. above the degraded coin. For the purpose of conveniently elucidating this subject, I propose to draw a distinction between the retail or trading currency, and the wholesale or commercial currency, — a distinction between trade and commerce without a lexical difference perhaps, and arbitrary withal, but yet essential to a clear presentation of the subject. Some writers consider that bills of exchange form a part of the currency, but the proposition cannot be admitted. Suppose A in Chicago, by means of his own check, purchases of the bank a bill of exchange on New York. What is the result ? A has reduced his deposit account, the bank has reduced its liability to A, and the bank in New York has reduced it liability to the bank in Chicago by reducing its balance, out of which the bill of exchange has been paid and passed out of existence; and the party in New York, from whom the bill of exchange was redeemed, has increased his deposit account. The bill of exchange, in this instance, was merely the agency by which a deposit was transferred from A in Chicago to the payee in New York. No additional deposit was created; the aggregate deposits in the country remained the same. Suppose A, instead of giving his check for the bill of exchange in Chicago, had handed bank-notes. Without stopping to inquire where A procured the notes, it will be sufficient to say that the active circulation of the country was, for the moment, reduced so much, and the deposits in New York were increased so much, if the proceeds of the bill of exchange had been credited to the deposit account of the payee, as we have supposed was the case. If the payee received bank-notes in payment, then the active circulation was increased at New York and decreased at Chicago, the circulation in the aggregate remaining the same. The aggregate circulation and deposits of the country were not changed in either case; only the bank balances were reduced. If, however, the bill of exchange was drawn on time, and the payee had merely procured acceptance thereof, and locked it in his safe, then the circulation and deposits having been decreased in Chicago, without being increased in New York, the net result is a diminution of the aggregate circulation and deposits in the country. The character of the transaction effected by the bill of exchange, is the transfer of currency by proxy, as it were, which is in essence the same as a telegraphic or manual transfer. Clearly then, bills of exchange are not currency. Fictitious exchange may be created thus. If A in Chicago wishes to obtain money, he draws on B in New York at thirty days and sells the bill in Chicago, which B in New York accepts ; at, or near maturity, A will draw on C in New York for the same amount *plus* interest, and send the bill to B, which B will have accepted and discounted, and with the proceeds will meet the first bill, and so on. In this case, no addition to the currency is made until B gets the second bill drawn on C discounted at a bank, thus creating a deposit, against which he draws his check to meet the first bill. Then the addition to the currency is made by creating a deposit in the bank, and the bank will add to its resources by loans and discounts, and increase its liabilities by deposits, and the currency of the country (circulation and deposits) becomes increased. But the bill of exchange, by itself, is not currency any more than a promissory note, or government bonds, or anything else upon which the bank may have loaned. This practice of drawing and redrawing is justly condemned by Adam Smith, and is similar to what is technically known in finance as making paper. If, however, A was possessed of merchandise not already hypothecated, and equal in value to the amount of the bill of exchange, the transaction was legitimate. Nor are foreign bills of exchange currency, in any sense. Foreign exchange is drawn against commodities in transit, and is the same in effect as if A telegraphed to B, to pay C in London, and charge to consignment of cotton, per "Friendship," bill of lading and invoice per mail. In case the exchange is drawn against bullion or coin, it is the same thing. Bullion is a commodity, and so is coin which loses the form of currency, and becomes a commodity only, when it leaves its native shores. I have dwelt on this subject because it has been involved in some obscurity. Bank balances have no effect upon the volume of the currency; if obliterated, the volume of the currency would remain the same; the debts are set off against the credits, and being payable in current funds on demand, thus neutralize each other.   Bank balances, however, are exceedingly prejudicial to the stability of debit banks at the commercial centre, in the inception of a revulsion.[1]   Nor do bank reserves constitute any portion of the working currency, whether they consist of specie or lawful money.   They ought to be composed entirely of lawful money under the present system, for specie is no more fit to exercise a salutary influence as a reserve, than would be so many bales of cotton of equal value.   Nor are compound interest notes, nor anything else that the banks would be reluctant to part with, except under a panic pressure, fit to be considered as a reserve.   The reserves of the banks are intended to perform very much the same office as that portion of an army which is held in reserve, during a battle, and which, if destitute of mobility, is worse than useless.

It is seen, then, that " the amount of the currency of a country dependent upon the movement of its banks, is to be found in the circulation and the deposits, *minus* the quantity of specie retained on hand,"[2] or whatever beside specie may be held as the reserve.   It is a matter of

---

[1] Walker.   [2] Carey and Walker.

much surprise that Professor Perry should dispute the proposition that deposits are a portion of the currency, and the very high character of his work justifies an examination into his reasons for disputing a point so well settled. His reason (1.) is, "Because so long as they remain unchecked there is no function of currency about them." The answer to this is, that they do not remain in the bank unchecked, but are constantly being transferred by check from one account to another. An active day in Wall Street will witness the transfer of millions, several times during business hours. (2.) "Because payments made by check do not cancel the debt at once, as when made by currency." The answer to this is, that if a check is good, it cancels a debt just as effectually as a good bank or legal tender note, and with more convenience, since checks can be drawn to a point for any fraction of a dollar. If a check is not good it will not cancel a debt; neither will a bank-note that is bad. (3.) "And because especially checks never perform but one of the functions of currency; they are provisionally a medium of exchange, but no matter how multitudinous they may become, or how actively they may pass in payments, there is no tendency whatever, as there would be in a corresponding increase of currency, to vary the meaning of the word dollar." This is the most important objection urged by Professor Perry, but it is fallacious. There can be no general inflation of prices, without increasing the circu-.lating notes or retail currency,[1] and this increase of retail or trading currency precedes, or follows, or accompanies an increase of loans and discounts, and consequently deposits, thus increasing the wholesale or commercial currency. The increase of deposits is as essential to a general inflation as an increase of circulating notes. Deposits are a demand liability of the banks in the same degree and kind as their circulating notes.

The following table shows the course of an inflation : —

Year.	Circulation.	Deposits.	Year.	Circulation.	Deposits.
1854	millions 205	187	1858	millions 155	· 186
1855	" 187	190	1859	" 193	259
1856	" 198	210	1860	" 207	253
1857	" 215	230			

[1] " The circulation of every country may be considered as divided into two branches ; the circulation of the dealers with one another, and the circulation between the dealers and the consumers. . . . . The value of the goods circulated between the different dealers, never can exceed the value of those circulated between the dealers and consumers."—*Smith*.

Mill is also very clear on this subject, quoting Tooke and Fullarton. Book iii. chap. xxiv.; also chap. xii.

It is thus seen that in theory and practice neither increase of circulation alone, nor of deposits alone, can materially affect prices or "vary the meaning of the word dollar," but an increase of both is essential to an inflation, and that each is a co-worker with the other. What I shall have to say upon the subject of interest, or the "charge for the use of money," may as well be said here as elsewhere. It is the vulgar theory, that the greater the quantity of the circulating medium, the lower the rate of interest in consequence.[1] This theory is also maintained by Mr. Carey, but Mr. Carey's whole theory of money, as well as interest, is at variance with that of all the known writers of reputation, I believe, without a single exception.[2] I cannot account for the eccentricity of Mr. Carey's views, except upon the hypothesis that he fails to determine the relation of cause and effect, throughout the whole course of his reasoning on the subject. It is not without deliberation and a sense of presumption, perhaps, that I venture so to express myself, but I must not shrink from the task I have undertaken, and in treating the

[1] This was John Law's theory.

[2] If it be said that Steuart, who preceded Smith, is an exception, I answer that his views, in the language of Say, "exhibit but a narrow and insignificant scope."

subject, I must observe the necessity of entire
candor. As a general rule, it may be stated that
the rate of interest depends upon the law of supply and demand. Money is circulating capital
in its greatest mobility of form, and it is capital
in its most convenient form that is needed when
money is borrowed. Money is no sooner received by the person borrowing, than he converts
it into some other form of capital, circulating or
fixed; and it is upon the profitable use made of
this latter that depends the fund out of which
interest is to be paid, with advantage to the borrower. Money is circulating capital, but all
circulating capital is not money; and the rate of
interest depends upon the supply of floating or
circulating capital to be loaned and the demand
for borrowing such capital. Money is only the
medium by which capital is transferred to the
borrower.[1] It is quite true that an inordinate
and sudden scarcity of money would necessitate
a high charge for its use until prices had become
generally affected by a considerable decline ; and
vice versa, an inordinate and sudden abundance of
money would create a low rate of interest until
prices had become generally affected by a con-

1 " It is, as it were, but the deed of assignment, which con-
veys from one hand to another those capitals which the
owners do not care to employ themselves." — *Smith*.

siderable advance. It must be borne in mind, however, that the value of the circulating medium of a nation is controlled by the international or universal laws of trade, or by the "equation of international demand." [1] This most important principle seems to have been ignored by Mr. Carey throughout. Without dwelling on this subject, it may be said the rate of interest depends, first, upon the supply, that is to say, the amount of accumulated capital seeking investment; second, upon the demand, which is created by various circumstances, — such as the profits of industry, the state of the societary circulation, the extension of the democratic principle in the body politic and the general distribution of wealth, the amount of the funded debt of the nation and the rate of interest thereon, rate of taxation and the wages of labor, and the material of the currency of a nation, whether of paper or otherwise. All these considerations, perhaps, have a bearing on the demand for the use of money, and there may be others which it were tedious and unnecessary to analyze. But the volume of currency, even if of gold, does

1 Mill, Perry, Bowen, Smith, Ricardo, Hume, Say, and others. Mill considers Ricardo as the real originator of this principle, but this is not so. The axiom laid down by Smith covers the whole ground, and contains the germ of the whole principle, in all its ramifications. *Post*, pp. 52, 65.

not, by any means, determine or affect the rate
of interest.

The instrument of association now in use is
constituted in a somewhat peculiar manner, upon
a basis of government paper money or bills of
credit, irredeemable promises to pay at some indefinite time in the future, but at present payable in nothing, otherwise than as they are received
for taxes, and whose circulation is therefore compulsory.　We are to deal with things as we find
them, and therefore it is not necessary to go into
an extended argument to show the necessity, or
otherwise, of the resort to a revolutionary currency when the war broke out.　It may be useful
to say, however, that when in the course of human events two opposing social forces close in
deadly conflict for the mastery ; when the civil
power of the · State is successfully resisted to
a degree which renders the existence of the
State itself contingent upon the fortune of
war ; when the foundations of society are over-
thrown and chaos reigns ; when the *habeas
corpus* is suspended and the laws are silent,
it needs but the issue of paper money to com-
plete the picture.　It is easy for so-called financiers, by ingenious arguments *a priori*, to show
that the issue of paper money is unnecessary

and therefore wrong; but history teaches that when bloody revolutions are undertaken, paper money is as necessary as powder and guns, and is, in fact, part of the *materiel* of civil war. History teaches that it always has been so, and political economy inculcates that it always will be so. Moreover, in our case, it was especially necessary, because, when the war broke out, the channels of circulation were choked up and overflowing with a paper currency, that was on the point of becoming inconvertible. It is one of the arguments in favor of a metallic circulation, that a nation possessing such is always on a war footing. The genius of republican liberty teaches that large standing armies are dangerous in time of peace; and the genius of political economy and republican liberty both teach that a bloated paper currency in time of peace is an unmitigated curse to society, likely to provoke civil strife, and always waging unrelenting war against the industry of the people. The component parts of the instrument of association may be described and enumerated as follows: —

April 1, 1868.	Plain legal tender notes	.	$356,144,727.00
	National bank-notes in circulation	. . .	295,017,089.00
	State bank-notes in circulation		3,310,177.00
			$654,471,993,00

Amount brought forward $654,471,993.00
Individual and other deposits of national banks   556,399,480.76
_____
1,210,871,473.76
Deduct actual legal tender reserve [1] 83,926,780.00
_____
Total depending on the government and national banks 1,126,944,693.76
To which must be added currency equivalent of gold certificates of deposits . .   24,838,884.00
_____
$1,151,783,577.76
_____

Deposits of State banks throughout the country, exclusive of the Pacific and gold-producing States, estimated [2] . . $100,000,000

Circulation of California, and other gold-producing States, according to the report of the Comptroller of the Currency, November, 1867, in gold coin $50,000,000

Estimated bank deposits in those States . 50,000,000
_____
$100,000,000 $\left\{ \begin{array}{c} \text{currency} \\ \text{value} \end{array} \right\}$ 140,000,000 [3]
_____
$240,000,000

[1] The reserve of the national banks is composed of compound interest notes, coin, three per cent. certificates, bank balances, and legal tenders. The amount given here was plain legal tender notes.

[2] I have no accurate data for this estimate; but the deposits of the State banks of New York alone on Dec. 28, 1867, were $32,957,573. The total of $100,000,000, is probably an under-estimate.

[3] This total is perhaps over-estimated, though, if the population of those States be three millions, it probably is not.

The nominal value of circulation and deposits throughout the country, is thus seen to be $1,151,783,577.76, + $240,000,000, equal to a total of $1,391,783,577.76; or, estimating the population at 35,000,000,[1] equal to a *per capita* total of about forty dollars in currency value. The instrument of association, then, is composed of mixed elements equal in currency value to about forty dollars *per capita*. In the next chapter I shall attempt to show the value of this instrument, as estimated in the common currency of the commercial world. It will be observed that the fractional currency is omitted from the above, for the special reason that it supplies the place of the gold and silver that was carried about in the pockets of the people before the war.[2] This amount prior to the war was an unknown quantity, and if we make a due allowance

[1] The Director of the Bureau of Statistics in 1866, estimated the population at 34,505,882, a gain of about ten per cent. in six years.

[2] The official estimates of the gold in the country in 1861 were $275,000,000. It would be interesting to know the basis of this estimate. The banks held less than $90,000,000 ; the people, perhaps, $30,000,000. Where was the remainder? It is possible that the estimate included the gold used in the arts, and regarded it as still in the country. It seems preposterous to suppose that there was so much gold coin in the country.

for increased prices now, it will perhaps be conceded that the nominal value of this fractional
currency is probably greater than the value of
the gold and silver which constituted that unknown quantity, especially as the small note circulation · before the war was abundant.   The
amount of fractional currency was $32,588,-
689.94.   Most extravagant estimates have been
made of this portion of the currency.   It con-
stitutes a part of the instrument of association,
and bears a uniform proportion to the general
currency, and is therefore thrown' out as not being material.   The circulating notes and deposits,
less the reserve, are, for the purpose of this dis-
cussion, sufficient to be considered as constituting
the instrument of association.

III.

THE PRINCIPLES OF POLITICAL ECONOMY WHICH LIMIT ITS VALUE.

IT is a self-evident proposition that there is some limit to the value of the instrument of association, whether the circulation consist of coin or of paper, which is fixed by some unwritten law that is superior to statute law, and which cannot be set aside by legislative enactment.   The very idea of value may be expressed by the word scarcity.   It is quite obvious that Congress cannot authorize the unlimited issue of bills of credit, without impairing their individual value, and finally their aggregate value, if the issue be carried to a great extent.   There is a point at which depreciation begins, another where it ends in absolute worthlessness, and intermediate points throughout the gamut in the scale of depreciation.   It is easy to define, with tolerable accuracy, the point at which depreciation commences, and it is here where the demoralization of society and the decay of industry begins.   " All increase of money beyond

this point, which the very nature of money itself
marks out as the boundary, leads to an inevitable
depreciation of the whole mass, to a consequent
disturbance of all existing money contracts, to
a universal rise of prices which are illusory and
gainless, to unsteadiness and derangement in all
legitimate business, and to a spirit of restless
enterprise and speculation, which seeks to draw
off the excess of money in untried and reckless
experiments." [1] It is not so easy, however, to define the point where depreciation ends, because
such a currency is commonly discarded by the
people before the issue has reached the point of
nothingness in value; for the moment that depreciation and fluctuations begin, the instrument is
impaired, and as the fluctuations grow wider the
instrument becomes useless, although its compo-
nents parts may not be without value.   In practice, a paper money currency is intolerable long
before it becomes without value in theory, that
is to say, on the basis of supply.   The value of
any commodity is limited by the cost of repro-
duction. [2]   This axiom is true when applied to a
metallic currency, because coin is a commodity
possessing a value independent of that which
it derives from the fact of its being the instru-

[1] Perry.   [2] Carey.

ment of association. Paper money, on the other
hand, derives value from one fact only — that of
its being the instrument of association.   But
the instrument of association, whether composed
of coin or paper, is limited in value, as I have
said before, by an unwritten law.   If it be
sought to increase the value of the instrument
of association, when composed of coin, beyond
the limit, the coin will flow out of the country,
or be used in the arts, or cease to be produced.
If it be sought to increase the value of the instrument of association, when composed of paper, beyond the limit, the paper must suffer depreciation.   The law which limits the value of
the instrument of association, is one of the most
important laws of political economy.[1]   It is also
a law which, I think, has received less attention
and elaboration than any other of equal impor-
tance.   It may be stated in the form of a syllogism thus: (1.) The money value or price of
the instrument of association, or wheel of circulation,[2] bears a certain proportion to the money
value or price of commodities which it is used
to circulate, and by a physical law it is confined

---

1 " Few writers since Ricardo have had an adequate con-
ception of the scientific value of this principle." — *Mill*, book
iii. chap. xxi.
    2 Smith.

within this limit.   This is a self-evident proposition. (2.) The average money value or price of
commodities within any nation, is regulated and
limited to the average money value or price of
commodities throughout the commercial world,
by the operations of international trade, anything
in the tax laws of any nation to the contrary notwithstanding.[1] (3.) Therefore, the money value
or price of the instrument of association within
any nation is independent of statute law, and is
fixed by the natural laws of trade, or by the
tides of commerce, or, as it were, by the law of
gravitation. The major premise of the syllogism
is, as I have stated, self-evident ; but it may be
said that the proportion of value borne by the
instrument of association, to the value of the
commodities circulated, has been variously estimated from one fifth to one thirtieth,[2] and a
recent writer has estimated it as low as one for-
tieth ;[3] but it is impossible to ascertain the values
exchanged in any community, and consequently
it is impossible to ascertain the ratio of value
borne by the medium of exchange, though, as
will be demonstrated hereafter, it is not difficult
to determine, very nearly, the approximate value

---

[1] " The equation of international demand, is the law of
international trade." — *Mill.*

[2] Smith and Say.   [3] Perry.

of the medium itself.   Whether the instrument
be of coin or paper, the premise is the same.
" England, in its actual state, requires, for the
effectuation of its sales and purchases, an agent
or medium equal in value, say to 1,284,000
pounds weight of gold ; or, what is the same
thing, to 1,200,000,000 pounds weight of sugar ;
or, what is still the same thing, to 60,000,000
pounds sterling of paper." [1] Now, if the proportion borne by the medium of exchange to the
products exchanged was, in value, as one to
thirty, then the value of the commodities exchanged was 1,800,000,000 pounds sterling.
Now, suppose the instrument of association to be
increased to 2,568,000 pounds weight of gold,
or to 2,400,000,000 pounds of sugar, or to
120,000,000 pounds sterling of paper, what is
the effect?   Simply that the wages of labor will
be doubled, and that the prices of all other commodities will be doubled, but the ratio of value
between the instrument and the commodities will
remain unchanged. [2] Two pounds weight of gold,
or two pounds weight of sugar, or two pounds
sterling of paper will purchase no more value
than would one pound of gold, or sugar, or pa-

[1] Say, in 1803.
[2] Prices will be doubled, but values will remain unchanged.

4

per before the change was made; and the price
of the total commodities exchanged would be
doubled as estimated against the medium of exchange, but as estimated against the wages of
labor, the value of the commodities would remain
unchanged.   It is quite true that rapidity of circulation is important to be considered; and hence,
if commodities of the value of 1,800,000,000
pounds sterling were to be circulated by 30,000,-
000 pounds sterling of paper, or 600,000,000
pounds weight of sugar, or 642,000 pounds
weight of gold, then the circulation must be twice
as rapid as when the medium of circulation was
twice as great, thus proving the axiom stated elsewhere, that the smaller the volume of the currency,
the more rapid the circulation, and the greater
the prosperity of the nation.[1] " If each piece of
money changes hands on an average ten times
while goods are sold to the value of a million
sterling, it is evident that the money required to
circulate those goods is £100,000." [2] It is important to preserve the distinction between money as
an instrument of commerce, and as a measure
of value. " There is the same difference between
money as a medium and money as a measure,
that there is between a bushel of wheat and that

1 *Ante*, p. 19.   2 Mill.

round thing by which we determine that there is
a bushel." [1] A bushel of wheat weighs about
sixty pounds ; but supposing that the use of two
measures, each denominated bushels, was made
compulsory in order to measure sixty pounds of
wheat, then, of course, two bushels of wheat
under the new rule are only equal to one bushel
under the old rule, and the medium of exchange
has depreciated fifty per cent., though the sixty
pounds of wheat as a measure of value is unchanged. It seems supererogatory to attempt
to demonstrate this premise any further, and
I pass on to the elucidation of the minor premise. It remains to demonstrate that the prices
of commodities within any nation are limited,
by the operations of international trade, to the
prices of corresponding commodities throughout
the commercial world. When the currency of
a nation is redundant, prices of commodities
are high, especially such as are the product
of labor, rather than the product of the soil; [2]
and the consequence is, that similar commodities produced within a nation where there
is a sound currency, and where they can
be produced at cheaper price, will inevitably
flow in to the highest market, and so continue,

---

[1] Perry.   [2] This is an important fact.

until the prices are equalized by a reduction of
the currency. *The rate of exchange is always
against that country which maintains a depreciated currency.*[1] This is an axiom. Any currency that is in excess of the prescribed limit, is
a depreciated currency, whether it consist of gold
or paper. It is wholly in vain that recourse is
had to the tariff to prevent the importation of
commodities, especially manufactured commodities ; for taxes, whether internal or external, so
far as they operate upon the cost of producing
any commodities within any nation, tend to enhance cost of production, and therefore do not
prevent importation. Suppose, for instance, that
woolen goods are barred out beyond the possi-
bility of smuggling. What is the consequence?
Why, the cost of home-made woolen goods is
immediately advanced by the law of supply and
demand, and the advance in these home-made
woolen goods is felt by the producers of domestic
cotton, linen, and silk goods ; and the productions

[1] Smith. It is not intended to say that the rate of exchange,
owing to the shipment of bonds and securities, may not be for
a time, and occasionally, in favor of a country which has a depreciated currency. The fact that bonds are shipped proves
the rule, rather. The balance of account on merchandise
transactions will always be against the nation whose currency
is redundant.

of iron and of the soil, and their products are
all enhanced in cost in consequence, until they,
in turn, become subjected to foreign competition.
Moreover, the government must have revenue,
and if it cannot collect from woolen goods, it
must collect from some other products, domestic
or foreign, which taxation must finally fall on
the producer of domestic commodities.[1]   " If by
any means one nation should obtain a larger portion of the whole currency of the world than
falls to it by the regular course of trade, all articles of merchandise belonging to that nation
must rise in price; they must be exchanged for
a larger quantity of money. Articles of foreign
growth and manufacture would be irresistibly
attracted thither by this alteration of values. A
single article might possibly be excluded by pro-
hibitory legislation. But no arbitrary enactments
can so clip the wings of commerce as to prevent
it from seeking a market in a country where the
prices of all commodities have risen above their
average value all the world over. Foreign goods
must necessarily be imported in such a case,
whether by open trading or by smuggling; and

---

[1] It is a mistake to suppose that all taxation does not finally
fall on the producer. An exception to this rule, however, is
noted hereafter.

being imported, they must be paid for. Money
is the only redundant article in such a community, the only one which can be offered in payment; for all other goods are, by the hypothesis,
of a higher price with them than in any other
country, and cannot be sent abroad but by a sac-
rifice.   Money, then, will be exported, in spite
of all coast guards, and even of the penalty of
death ; and the currency would thus be reduced
to its natural level."[1]   Money advances in value
as it declines in quantity, and declines in value
as it advances in quantity,[2] like anything else.
Money is not a commodity of which an unlimited quantity can be absorbed by business, but
is an instrument for a certain specific purpose.[3]
So are sewing-machines.[4]   Therefore, money
being for a certain specific purpose, that of ex-
changing commodities (it does not create commodities, on the contrary, it checks production,
when in excess[5]) already existing and waiting to
be exchanged, it follows that an increase of supply must decrease the value, in obedience to the
law of supply and demand.   So that, when
money is unduly increased in one country, it will
go abroad where it will be more appreciated.[6]

[1] Bowen.   [2] Say.   [3] Perry.   [4] Ibid.
[5] It temporarily stimulates trade.
[6] *Ante*, p. 20. Ricardo.

It therefore follows, that when prices are high in one country, commodities are imported, and money is exported, until the prices are equalized throughout the commercial world.[1]   The converse of this proposition is also true, namely, the value of the currency of any nation cannot remain below a certain point for a lengthy period, because commodities will fall in price and be exported, and money will be imported.   The lower the value of the currency of a nation, the more advantageous its foreign trade, showing again the truth of the axiom elsewhere stated.[2] I trust I have satisfactorily demonstrated. the minor premise of the syllogism, and the conclusion follows, — that the value of the instrument of association is fixed by natural law, and is wholly independent of legislation.

One of the most important principles of political economy having been demonstrated, it becomes a question how to apply it to the instrument of association in this country.   How shall we ascertain the value of the instrument of association as fixed by the natural laws of trade,

---

1 " If a country has more money than is sufficient to accomplish its exchanges, it sends it abroad, and receives back something that it needs more." — *Wayland.*

2 *Ante,* p. 19.

and what is that value? We have seen that the nominal value in paper of our currency is close upon $1,400,000,000,[1] and it is proposed by some to increase this nominal valuation. It is said occasionally, that the "opinion of some of our best financiers" is, that we have no more money than we need; and one of the leading metropolitan journals stated, that it preferred "to resume specie payments by a moderate expansion rather than by contraction." The premium on gold is no more a criterion of the value of the instrument of association, than the price of cotton, for gold is demonetized, and has become a commodity only, in the domestic market. Besides, it is higher now than when the volume of currency was greater, three years since, and is or has been governed by the caprice of one man. Nor are the wages of labor any criterion of the value of the instrument of association, for, compared with the cost of living and the precarious and unsteady character of the demand for labor, they are below what an industrious and honest man has a right to expect in this country. Political economy, as I have said, is an experimental science and deals with facts; it does not advance gratuitous assumptions; it has nothing to do with

[1] *Ante,* p. 43.

false premises and illogical conclusions. If Adam Smith were alive to-day, with more modesty than " our best financiers," [1] he would say, — Unless I turn to your history, I cannot form any opinion of what the value of your currency may be, because there is nothing upon which I can base an intelligent opinion ; but judging from the fact that, since the abandonment of the specie standard, besides exporting rather more than your gold product, you have accumulated an interest bearing debt to foreign nations of, perhaps, a thousand millions of dollars ; the gold value of your currency is maintained very much above its true value, and unless adjusted to its true value, you will be overtaken by the greatest catastrophe, considering its probable effects, that is yet recorded in history. Turning then to history, and beginning at the period when the influence of the accession of the precious metals from the mines of California and Australia was felt by the commercial world, it is seen that the value of the instrument of association is there defined with

---

[1] " The results of such an education were most disastrous to England, for there arose a race of so-called financiers ; — men who drew their political economy from the traditions of the Exchequer, and their financial knowledge from the Stock Exchange." — *British Finance in* 1816 : *N. A. Review,* April, 1867, Art. ii. p. 379.

marvelous accuracy.   Let the following table
show :

Year.	Cir. & Dep. Millions.	Cir. & Dep. *Per Capita.*	Specie Movement.	
			Net Import.	Net Export.
1849	$205	$9.18	$1,246,592	
1850	240	10.32		$2.894,202
1851	284	11.71		24,019,160
1852	328	13.38		37,169,091
1853	348	13.90		23,285,493
1854	392	15.25		34,478,272
1855	377	14.22		52,587,531
1856	408	14.90		41,537,853
1857	445	15.60		56,675,123
1858	341	11.56		33,358,651
1859	452	14.87		57,517,708
1860	460	14.84		57,996,104

By the foregoing table, the average *per capita* proportion of circulation and deposits, was
13\frac{68}{100}$ during the twelve years from 1849 to
1860 inclusive, and under this average, the entire product of the mines, excepting what was
consumed in the arts, has been exported.   In
1854, the annual product of the mines was not
only exported, but the specie reserves of the
bank were drawn on ; on the following year, the
banks made a small gain in the specie reserve,
and in 1856 they began to lose again, till in
1857 they were drawn down lower than they
were in 1837,[1] and the banks suspended specie

---

[1] In proportion to circulation.

payments. The incontestable — the historical fact then is, that the value of the instrument of association in this country is at the rate of $13\frac{68}{100}$ dollars *per capita;* and beyond this point the currency, whether it consist of coin or paper, becomes depreciated as estimated against the currency of the commercial world, and imports are greater than exports by the value of our gold product; [1] and if foreign nations do not take our gold product, we shall begin accumulating a debt. Estimating our population at 34,500,-000, the value of the instrument of association is $471,960,000, and whenever any addition is made to this value, the coin equivalent thereof must go abroad, or we must run in debt to foreign nations. This, I say, is the value in the common currency of the world, and if we go on and issue paper forever, the whole mass will be worth no more than this sum.[2] Why is this? Because the business of circulating all the values

---

[1] And in proportion as we exceed the limit, so is the excess of imports. If with gold at $1.40, the *per capita* is $30, or more than twice the limit, then the imports of merchandise must be more than twice the exports of merchandise. That is, if the exports of merchandise are, gold, $200,000,000, then the imports will be $400,000,000, or $200,000,000 in excess. If we export $50,000,000, gold, then we must create a debt of $150,000,000, gold. I state this as a general principle.

[2] John Adams.

of the United States requires no larger value.[1]
Of what value then is " the *opinion* of some of
our best financiers," in the face of these facts?
But the circumstances of the country are not the
same as they were, it may be said.   Granted;
but the circumstances of other countries are very
much the same, and it is the value of the common currency of the commercial world that limits the value of our currency.   But there has been
a general rise of prices throughout the commercial
world, it may be said.   Granted; but the agency
of steam and electricity, increase of book credits
and other expedients have so economized the use
of money, that no more *per capita* is required
than half a century since.   The circulation and
deposits of the Bank of England are no greater
per capita than thirty years ago.[2]   But we are
subjected to heavy taxation, and taxation tends to
enhance the cost of commodities, and therefore
we require a greater value to circulate those commodities.   The conclusive answer to this objec-

---

[1] Say.

[2] In 1836 it required $17.60 *per capita* to cause a revulsion,
and in 1856 it required only $15.60.   The genius of the age
tends to a less amount of money being employed as the instrument of association.   As wealth increases, more gold is used
in the arts and less for money.   " Proportion borne by money
to commerce, decreases in advancing countries." — *Carey.*

tion is, that the average prices of commodities in this country cannot rise above the average prices of commodities throughout the commercial world, and consequently, if taxation is increased, the wages of labor, rent, and profits[1] must be reduced.[2] If this were not so, manifestly there would be no limit to the ability of a nation to support taxation. If the consequence of taxation was the increase of prices merely, we could support any amount of taxation; but the moment that prices are increased beyond a certain limit, excessive importation results, production ceases, and labor starves. "The quantity of precious metals retained in circulation as coin, for the whole world, regulates itself through the aggregate amount of money actually needed by all mankind to effect their exchanges — regulates itself wholly irrespective of the efforts made by one government, or by all governments, to increase or diminish its amount."[3] Such is the inexorable law, — "Hitherto shalt thou come, but no further; and here shall thy proud waves be stayed."

[1] Smith.

[2] This is why taxation is finally paid by the producing classes.

[3] Bowen.

IV.

ON ITS ADJUSTMENT.

IF the circulation consist of coin, the instrument of association will be self-adjusting; but if the circulation consist of bills of credit, whether the exigency which called them forth be passed or not, the instrument must be adjusted by the sovereign power, or bankruptcy, — the universal bankruptcy of the people, accompanied perhaps by civil strife,[1] will become a question of time only. In order to effect the adjustment of the instrument it is necessary, first, to examine its condition. The value of the instrument of association in the United States does not exceed about $13\frac{68}{100}$ dollars of the common currency of the world *per capita*, or in the lump, about $500,000,000, or about £100,000,000 as a *maximum*.[2] This is its value, fixed, not by us, but in spite of us, by a law over which neither

---

[1] Shay's Rebellion and the " Reign of Terror " were caused by paper money.

[2] *Ante*, p. 58, or little more than 2,000,000 pounds, troy weight, of pure gold.

this nor any other nation exercises the slightest control. The value in paper, as we have seen,[1] is about $1,400,000,000, and by maintaining the price of gold at $1.40, the artificial price (*not value* in the common currency of the world),[2] or gold weight, is about $1,000,000,000. With the price of gold at $2.80, the gold weight of the instrument will be reduced to its true *maximum* value — $500,000,000 in the currency of the world. It is here necessary to repeat an axiom elsewhere stated [3] (and I ask careful attention, else my proposition will be regarded a paradox), laid down by Say, to wit: *Money advances in value as it declines in quantity, and declines in value as it advances in quantity.*[4] In other words, as the gold weight of our paper instrument increases, so it becomes unwieldy and depreciated as an instrument of association. Suppose that our circulation were coin instead of paper. Then the circulation and deposits would be $1,400,000,000 in gold weight, and estimated against the wages of labor, would be more depre-

---

1 *Ante*, p. 43.

2 The common currency of the world is gold, but gold that will purchase more labor than American gold will in the United States.

3 *Ante*, p. 54.

4 The idea is not Say's own, but the language merely.

ciated than now.[1] I crave attention then to the very important proposition, that *the value of the instrument of association is inversely as its gold weight, and the depreciation of the instrument of association is vice versa, directly as its gold weight.* It is not that, our circulation and deposits being \$1,400,000,000 in *paper*, the exchange with foreign nations is, in consequence, against us; but it is because the *gold* weight of our circulation and deposits is \$1,000,000,000, that exchange is against us. If the gold weight of our circulation and deposits does not exceed \$500,000,000, our merchandise transactions will balance each other by the aid of the export of our gold product, and we shall cease to run in debt. It will be seen that, with the average of \$13 $\frac{68}{100}$ *per capita*, our gold product was exported, so that if the gold value of our circulation and deposits now be \$13 $\frac{68}{100}$, the currency will be restored to its ante-war value. I ought to state that \$500,000,000 is the true *maximum* value of the instrument of association. If we wish to turn the exchange in our favor, so as to accumulate gold wherewith to establish a sound currency, then we must contract the in-

---

[1] Under such circumstances our export trade would be brought nearly to a halt.

strument of association below the measure of $500,000,000 gold. Our legal tender notes, in themselves, convey no definite idea of value at all;[1] whatever value they possess, accrues to them from the fact that they form the materials of the instrument of association, and the value of the instrument of association cannot exceed, at present, $500,000,000 gold. If, by reason of drawing gold from the people by taxes, and selling it, the value of the instrument is nominally enhanced to $1,000,000,000, the enhanced value is apparent only, for the real and true result is that the gold itself is depreciated fifty per cent. ; and as *the exchange is always against that country which maintains a depreciated currency*,[2] it results that as a nation we are owing a demand debt of a thousand millions of dollars,[3] with interest thereon at the rate of six per cent. per annum, besides having exported the annual gold product. The nation has been consuming more than it has been producing even since the war closed, and taxation is encroaching upon capital, and we seem to be approaching the abyss of bankruptcy, slowly, perhaps, but yet surely.

---

[1] Say.   [2] Smith.

[3] It is not probable that this estimate is excessive. As between commercial nations, these bonds constitute a demand debt.

Was ever the insensate folly of empiricism attended by more disastrous results? It seems to me that the administration of our fiscal affairs has been profligate beyond any possible parallel. I know not whether the people will ever realize the truth of our terrible financial situation in time to prevent a great catastrophe; but I believe that, sooner or later, they will learn to execrate the authors of a policy which has impoverished thirty millions of people, and brought disgrace upon their cherished name and fame among the nations of the earth.

The adjustment of the instrument of association consists in establishing its value to the sum of $500,000,000 gold, or less, in order to turn the exchange in our favor. There is only one method by which this adjustment can be made. It is the popular idea that the currency can and must be contracted or funded, until the circulation and deposits are reduced to the nominal limit.[1] Can this be done? I lay it down as a law of political economy, that the currency can neither be contracted nor funded, and that the attempt to do either will ruin the debtor classes, destroy the cap-

---

[1] This seems to be the idea of Secretary McCulloch. It may also be entertained by many others, but a little reflection will suffice to dispel it.

ital of the banks, national and state; it will destroy the value of the public securities and the credit of the nation, and perhaps cause the overthrow of the government itself. I lay it down as a law of political economy, that our paper money is worth about thirty-three cents on the dollar, and that it is as impossible to restore this currency to the value of one hundred cents on the dollar, as to transmute one third of a dollar's worth of gold into one dollar's worth of gold. It does not represent sufficient value. *Facilis descensus.*[1] It is easy to take from that which is, but it is impossible to take from that which is not. There is not an instance in history where government paper money once issued to excess, has ever been contracted or funded, nor is it likely there will be. Nay, more, I lay it down as a law of political economy, that if the present condition of the instrument of association be

[1] . . . . Facilis descensus Averno ;
Noctes atque dies patet atri janua Ditis :
Sed revocare gradum, superasque evadere ad auras,
Hoc opus, hic labor est.

The currency is precisely in the same condition as if the circulation were coin, and the coin had been clipped from time to time, so that two thirds had been clipped away, leaving only one third of the original coin to represent a dollar, and this third made a legal tender. The deceit is perfect: the value has disappeared.

maintained ; if the government is able to maintain the price of the legal tender notes at seventy cents when their value is thirty-three cents, and persists in so doing, it will have to make additional issues from time to time,' or the people will starve. I mean to say that if the government wishes to maintain the price of the currency above its value, then it must supply the people from the printing-press ; for the industry of the people will not enable them to supply themselves. I do not, of course, expect the people will starve, but I expect the present status must be radically changed, or the people will demand a further issue ; and if any party attempts to stand in the way of their necessities, it will be their right and duty to assert their sovereign power. Towards the close of the French Revolution "the arbitrary government of the Jacobins, who were then in power, having put in forced circulation the anticipated proceeds of the property,[1] now undertook to sustain the value of its currency by penal enactments. They might as well have enacted laws to prevent the sun from setting at the close of the day. Six years' imprisonment was denounced against any one who should exchange

[1] In this country it is the anticipated proceeds of the public revenue which is exhausting the people.

any amount of silver or gold for a greater nominal value of *assignats*; and a *maximum* of price
was established for bread and the other necessa-
ries of life.   The only consequence was, that the
owners of grain and other commodities refused to
bring them to market at all, and thus what was
a scarcity became a famine.   The starving people then became furious; the severities formerly
exercised only against the nobles, the clergy,
and the royalists, were now turned against the
rich, the farmers of the public revenue, the trad-
ers, who were accused of monopolizing food and
holding it back from sale; and these were sent in
crowds to the guillotine.   But all the terrors of
that period, which was emphatically called the
' Reign of Terror,' were not enough to arrest the
depreciation." [1]   The attempt to conceal the depreciation of the paper currency in this country
by making it command a certain quantity of
gold, is much more reprehensible than the attempt
of the French Jacobins to make their currency
command a certain quantity of bread; it probably
will not be followed by such bloody consequences
as those which marked French history, but it
will be succeeded by very unpleasant results,
equally fatal to public credit; it is more insidious,

[1] Bowen.

and, therefore, more dangerous. The French *assignats* were finally made exchangeable into *mandats*, at the rate of thirty for one ; but the *mandats* became as much depreciated as the *assignats* before them, and by a spasmodic effort the currency was discarded.[1]   A feeble attempt was made by the Continental Congress to take up the paper money by issuing notes of new tenor, at the rate of forty of old tenor for one of new tenor; but the attempt failed, and finally the bills ceased to circulate.[2]   It is probable that both the *assignats* and Continental bills had some value on the basis of supply, but as constituting the instrument of association they were worthless, for the fluctuations were so constant and violent, that it was impossible to tell one moment how much bread could be purchased the next moment with the same bill.[3]   Austria retired its bills of credit that were issued during the Napoleonic wars, by issuing notes of redemption at the rate of five of old to one of new ; but the old notes were over-estimated in value, so that the notes of redemption were, in fact, depreciated when issued, and they had to be taken up at the reduced rate

---

[1] Bowen.
[2] Hildreth, vol. iii. chap. xlvi.
[3] *Ante*, p. 46.

of forty cents on the dollar.[1] It is probable, perhaps, that had Austria issued its new notes of redemption at the rate of seven or eight for one, the expedient would have been successful. In a measure of this kind, great care must be taken not to over-estimate the value of the old currency that is to be disposed of, otherwise the expedient will not be successful; on the other hand, if it be under-valued, no harm can arise, because coin will flow into and fill any vacuum in the channels of circulation. Russia, after suffering from excessive issues of paper money that were made during the Napoleonic wars, fixed their value in 1839, by making them convertible into notes of the Commercial Bank of St. Petersburgh, at the rate of four to one,[2] and now their value is fixed at the rate of three and one half paper roubles for one silver rouble.

The history of England, during the bank restriction from 1797 to 1821, is interesting and instructive. I shall quote from one of the best and most intelligent authorities on the subject.[3] " The year 1797 is, however, the most important epoch in the recent history of the bank. Owing partly to events connected with the war in which

---

[1] Hulburd, Comptroller of the Currency, 1867.
[2] Ibid.   [3] McCulloch.

we were then engaged — to loans to the Emperor of Germany — to bills drawn on the treasury at home by the British agents abroad — and partly and chiefly, perhaps, to the advances most unwillingly made by the bank to government, which prevented the directors from having sufficient control over their issues — the exchanges became unfavorable in 1795,[1] and in that and the following year large sums in specie were drawn from the bank. In the latter end of 1796 and beginning of 1797, considerable apprehensions were entertained of invasion, and rumors were propagated of descents having been actually made on the coast. In consequence of the fears that were thus excited, runs were made on the provincial banks in different parts of the country; and some of them having failed, the panic became general, and extended itself to London. Demands for cash poured in upon the bank from all quarters; and on Saturday, the 25th of February, 1797, she had only £1,272,000 of cash and bullion in her coffers, with every prospect of a violent run taking place on the following Monday. In this emergency an order in council was issued on Sunday, the 26th, prohibiting the

---

[1] That is to say, the currency became depreciated, and the exchange turned against England.

directors from paying their notes in cash until
the sense of Parliament had been taken on the
subject. And after Parliament met, and the
measure had been much discussed, it was agreed
to continue the restriction till six months after
the signature of a definitive treaty of peace."
Such were the events preceding the restriction.
The issues of the bank were so moderate, however, that during the first three years they sometimes bore a small premium; but in the latter
part of 1800, they fell to about 8 per cent. discount, as compared with gold; then rose again,
soon after, nearly to par, and so continued till
1809, when, owing principally to increased issues of country banks, they fell to $13\frac{1}{2}$ per cent.
discount; then, mostly in consequence of dimin-
ished volume of country bank issues, rose to
about 8 per cent. discount; then, owing to increased issues both of Bank of England and
country banks, they rapidly depreciated to a little
more than 25 per cent. discount in 1814; so that
in the middle of the year 1814, the circulation
of the Bank of England was £28,979.876, and
that of the country banks £22,709,000, or
both combined, £51,688,876. At this point it
will be useful to resume the narrative. "But
the harvest of that year (1813) being unusually

productive, and the intercourse with the Conti
nent being then also renewed, prices, influenced
by both circumstances, sustained a very heavy
fall in the latter part of 1813, and the beginning
of 1814.[1]   And this fall having proved ruinous
to a considerable number of farmers, and produced a general want of confidence, such a
destruction of provincial paper took place as has
rarely been paralleled.   In 1814, 1815, and
1816, no fewer than 240 country banks stopped
payment; and *eighty-nine* commissions of bankruptcy were issued against these establishments,
being at the rate of one commission against every
ten and a half of the total number of banks existing in 1813.   The great reduction that had
been thus suddenly and violently brought about
in the quantity of country bank paper, by ex-
tending the field for the Bank of England paper,
raised its value, in 1817, nearly to a par with
gold.   The return to cash payments being thus
facilitated, it was fixed in 1819, by the act 59
Geo. III. c. 78, commonly called Mr. Peel's Act,

---

[1] Mr. Carey says that the revulsion in England was started
by the Bank of England, but I find no evidence that such
was the fact.   The circulation and deposits of the bank were
nearly eight millions sterling greater in August, 1814, than at
the same period in the previous year.

that they should take place in 1823." [1] In point
of fact, specie payments were resumed May 1,
1821, and in that year the circulation of the
Bank of England was £20,327,740, and that of
the country banks, £8,414,281, or both combined, £28,741,921. Judging from history, the
consequences of the wholesale destruction of
country bank paper, and the failure of these
banks, was well-nigh appalling. And the final
reëstablishment of the standard that existed in
1797, was one of the " most remarkable measures of confiscation to be found in the annals
of legislation." [2] The Comptroller of the Currency takes a very superficial view therefore, in
saying, — " With a sturdy good sense, however,
that did credit to their national character, the
English people set themselves to work to retrace
their steps, and after years of struggling and
suffering, the Bank of England again resumed
specie payments, but not until the paper currency had been reduced by the withdrawal of
£43,467,978." [3] The historical *fact* is, that the

1 McCulloch.   2 Carey.
3 Hulburd, 1867. " How far this depreciation was the cause
of speculation and over-trading, it is difficult to prove. It is,
however, agreed, that there was a very considerable rise in
prices from 1812 to 1814, and that country bankers undertook
to do more business than their capital justified on security that

combined circulation of the Bank of England
and the country banks never reached fifty-two
millions sterling at any time during the restriction, and the decrease in the combined circulation, when resumption took place, was less than
twenty-three millions sterling.   It seems almost
travesty, therefore, to characterize the indiscrimi-
nate robbery as something creditable to the good
sense of the British people.   There are two
points that force themselves on our attention, in
reviewing the experience of England.   First,
it is obvious that nothing of the kind can occur
here, since the government is responsible for the
whole circulation.   Second, if a reduction of
forty-five per cent. of the circulation caused such
destruction of property in England,[1] what would

was of too fluctuating a value to be safe. The consequence
was, that when, in 1814 and 1815, a reaction took place, first of
all in the price of corn, and then in that of almost every staple
article of trade, there ensued a crash among the private bankers, accompanied by a collapse of their credit as banks of
issue, which at once purged the circulation of a vast amount
of paper, and substituted that of the Bank of England in its
place.   But the relief thus given to the currency showed itself toward the close of 1816 by the restoration of the Bank
paper to a par with gold." — *British Finance in* 1816: *N. A.
Review,* April, 1867, Art. II. pp. 376, 377.

[1] The mischief in England was all done in 1814, 1815, and
1816, by a reduction of less than twenty per cent. of the circulation. The revulsion in 1857, in the United States, effected
a reduction of only twenty-five per cent. in the circulation.

be the probable effect of the reduction of sixty-five per cent. of the circulation in this country, even if it were possible? It would be of no avail to attempt to distribute this reduction over a series of years. If done at all, it must be done at one fell swoop, without regard to the political consequences, or the inconceivable sufferings of the people.

The instrument of association, as stated elsewhere,[1] is substantially composed of paper money, about equally divided between national bank circulation and legal tender notes. It is necessary to examine the national bank system in order to arrive at the object of our inquiry, — the adjustment of the instrument of association. It is probable that the abolishment of the old state banks of issue, and the establishment of the national banks under government auspices and control, in giving the government exclusive control of the channels of circulation, was an indispensable measure of safety, both for the Union and the people. It was necessary to the success of the government, that it should obtain and hold possession of the channels of circulation, otherwise the country would have been deluged with irredeemable paper, and the financial ruin of the

[1] *Ante*, p. 40.

nation completed at a very early stage of the war. That the state banks of issue could have been abolished, without something being offered in lieu thereof, may well be doubted, for even the establishment of the national banks met with a most determined opposition, notwithstanding the pecuniary advantages of the system. As *a war measure* at a critical period, the supersedure of the state banks of issue, by national banks of issue whose circulation was controlled and limited by the central power, must be regarded as an act of signal, and, probably, of saving advantage. There is no elasticity to this national bank circulation, and considering the inutility of its reserves,[1] and the fact of its inconvertibility into anything but bills of credit, it seems to be a hybrid, produced from interest bearing and non-interest bearing certificates of government indebtedness, in the composition of which the interest bearing element largely predominates. Stripped of the cobwebs that have been sedulously thrown about it,[2] this national bank circulation takes from the producing classes every year, about $15,000,000 net,[3] and is

---

[1] *Ante,* p. 34.

[2] The Comptroller showed that the banks actually were the losers of five and one half millions. 1867.

[3] Interest on circulation, less tax, and interest on plain legal

therefore a tax to that extent. But perhaps the worst feature of it is, that, instead of being under control of Congress, Congress seems to be controlled by the national banks. In the present condition of the country, therefore, and in view of the pressure of taxation upon all branches of industry, it seems to be a criminal act to surrender the channels of circulation, or any portion thereof, to any banks of issue, whether organized under state or federal laws. If the privilege of circulating notes were not immensely profitable, it would not be contested; being profitable, the profit should enure to the benefit of the tax-payers.[1] "If paper currency is to be substituted for metallic currency, the profits of the substitution ought to accrue for the benefit of those who make it — of those who are willing to give up coin, and accept paper with all its attendant risks. The act of substitution is the act of the community at large; to be the agents in this act is a usurped function of the banks, in no wise

tender reserve. As banks of deposit, the national banks are properly taxed, but as banks of issue, the privilege of circulating notes is worth about $15,000,000 net, which comes out of the people.

[1] The saving effected by abolishing the national bank circulation and substituting legal tender notes in place thereof, will be equal to a reduction of one per cent. in the income tax.

connected with their other and proper offices. It belongs to the state, and ought to be exercised for the benefit of the tax-payers — that is, of the persons who, by giving up coin and accepting paper, make a saving of the precious metals, and ought to profit by that saving." [1]   In order to adjust the present instrument of association to its proper value and efficiency, it will be important to displace the national bank-notes, and substitute legal tender notes in their place.[2]   This done, the repeal of the legal tender act should follow, with a provision that all existing debts, public and private, that were contracted in paper money, shall be paid in paper money, unless there is some existing law or agreement to the contrary. Lastly, the government shall issue notes of redemption, or specie notes, payable in specie on demand, into which the legal tenders shall be converted at the rate of three dollars of legal tender for one dollar of specie notes,[3] and the legal tenders shall be thereafter cancelled and

[1] Mill and Bowen. The language is Bowen's.

[2] This will release the legal tender reserve of the banks, and so add to the circulation and deposits, probably bringing the nominal value of the instrument of association up above $1,500,000,000, and it is this fact which necessitates great care not to overvalue the legal tenders.

[3] Existing debts due in paper money to be cancelled by specie notes at the rate of one for three of legal tenders.

destroyed. This is the only method of disposing of our paper money, without injury to the people, or danger to public credit. There are, I may safely say, but two ways of disposing of an excessive issue of bills of credit. One method is that already suggested. The other method, is to resort to continuous issues, till the whole fabric explodes, leaving a misgoverned and ruined people to mourn over the imbecility of their chosen and trusted servants. History may be searched in vain for any exception to the law here laid down. It is useless to argue that it should not be so, or that it need not be so. History teaches that it always has been so, and we may be assured that it always will be so.

6

V.

THE EFFECT OF THE ADJUSTMENT.

THE instant effect of the adjustment of the instrument of association to its normal weight of about 2,013,888 pounds troy, of pure gold, or about 2,239,583 pounds troy, of standard or coin gold, or about $500,000,000 in coin, will be to restore prosperity to all branches of industry throughout every section of the country; and if this adjustment be permanent, that is to say, if, having fixed the value of our paper money at three dollars for one dollar of coin, there be no further issues of paper money, either by banks or by government, the industry of the country will know no relaxation from its prosperous condition.[1] The average wages of labor, rent, and profits, will be restored to their most prosperous ante-war basis, less the difference between the present and ante-war taxa-

[1] I assume that there will be no tariff legislation hostile to industry.

tion.[1] Not only that, but the gold value of taxation will be reduced, even if the public securities
remain untaxed at their present rate of interest,
because the gold value of the expenses of the
federal and the municipal governments will
be reduced very largely. It may be useful to
repeat the principle upon which the instrument
of association is adjusted. (1.) The average
prices of commodities are equalized throughout
the commercial world by the operations of
international trade. (2.) The gold weight, or
money value of the instrument of association,
or the money value needed to circulate money
values, bears a fixed ratio to the money values
circulated. (3.) Therefore, if the average prices
or money values of commodities within any nation are regulated by the natural laws of trade,
then the money value of the instrument of association is regulated by the natural laws of trade.
And when the natural laws of trade are no
longer obstructed by empirical devices, the country will derive the utmost benefit from its un-
bounded natural resources. I have said that the
prosperity of the country would know no relaxa-
tion. The reason is, that when the instrument
of association is adjusted to its normal value,

[1] *Ante*, p. 61.

and further issues of paper are prevented, it is
obvious that any addition to the instrument of
association will require value; and value is the
product of labor rather than the product of legislation, and will not remain where it has become
superfluous or depreciated, but will go where
it will command the most value in exchange.
Therefore, if the currency be a currency of value, it will remain at or near the *minimum;* and
since it is a law that the smaller the value of the
instrument of association, the greater the prosperity of the nation,[1] it follows that with a currency of value, the prosperity of the nation will
be uniform and assured. The instrument of association in this country has never been composed of self-adjusting material, nor has there
been any effectual control over its nominal paper value ; consequently, the prosperity of the
country has been subjected to constant and un-
expected vicissitudes. People have become afflu-
ent from no merit or sagacity of their own, and
others have become impoverished through no
fault of their own. It is the inevitable effect of
any currency which is not a currency of value,
that " it enriches without merit, and ruins without

[1] *Ante*, p. 19.

blame." [1]   The currency *per capita* of the country for twenty-five years previous to the war,
varied from 6\frac{18}{100}$ to 17\frac{61}{100}$.   From 1849 to
1860, it varied from 9\frac{13}{100}$ to 15\frac{60}{100}$,[2] consequently there has been no uniform prosperity, no
social concord, no domestic tranquillity.[3]   It is
the vulgar opinion that a rise in the premium on
gold will cause a corresponding rise in the currency prices of all domestic commodities.   I say,
such is the vulgar opinion, because it is the
opinion of the uneducated and unreflecting mind.
It is also the vulgar opinion that high currency
prices are injurious, whereas there can hardly be
anything more remote from the truth.   The paper money prices of domestic commodities are
not regulated by the international laws of trade,
but by the quantity of paper money in use, and
by the condition of the societary circulation.
The law of supply and demand regulates price,
but the elements of supply consist of the supply
of commodities and the supply of paper money
in which the price is expressed.   It should be
remembered that our paper money is of forced
circulation, that it is the floating debt of the
government bearing no interest, and payable at

---

[1] Walker.   [2] *Ante*, p. 58.
[3] There has been a constant tariff war.

some indefinite time in the future, consequently, be its quantity more or less, it will all be used to circulate whatever commodities are circulated; and no more than is in circulation can be used to circulate whatever commodities are circulated; therefore, a rise in the currency price of gold will have no natural or great effect on the average price of domestic commodities. There will be a wholesome rise of prices, and this is what the people need. They need high currency prices, and low currency taxes. But unless the supply of currency be increased, there can be no great rise in currency prices. Whatever rise takes place, will be due to increased momentum of the currency, to increased activity of the societary circulation, and consequently, the higher currency prices rise, the more prosperous will be the people, provided such rise comes from an increased demand for commodities, and not from an increased supply of currency. Such a rise in currency prices will be evidence of increased production and consumption, and interchange of domestic commodities, creating an increased demand for the domestic currency; and consequently, as the demand for domestic currency increases, the exchangeable value of this domestic currency is prevented from going below a certain point, or, in other words, currency prices cannot advance beyond a certain point, if the supply of currency be fixed. The important point to be gained is the adjustment of commercial relations with the external world; and the adjustment of the instrument of association, as measured by the common currency of the world, will adjust those relations. The smaller the value or gold weight of the instrument of association, the more we shall sell and the less we shall buy of foreign nations. The greater the value or gold weight of the instrument of association, the more we shall buy and the less we shall sell to foreign nations. If the gold weight of the instrument of association exceed $500,000,000 coin, we shall buy from foreign nations more than we can pay for, and shall give to them evidences of debt (bonds), bearing interest, instead of value, in exchange for value; and so long as the value or gold weight remains in excess of $13\frac{68}{100}$ *per capita*, the process will go on *ad infinitum*. The average price of domestic commodities cannot rise materially, in consequence of a rise in the price of gold. There are some domestic commodities, however, that will be affected more than others, especially cotton. At, or above the cost of production, the price of cotton is regulated by

the price in England, the chief consuming country.   As an axiom, it may be laid down that at
or above the cost of production, the price of any
staple commodity is regulated by the market of
the chief consuming country; and that at or below the cost of production, the price of any staple commodity is regulated by the market of
the chief producing country.   In other words,
the demand is regulated by the chief consuming
country, and the supply, by the chief producing
country, and supply and demand govern price.
Consequently, the adjustment of the instrument
of association at the rate of three for one, will
enable the cotton producers of this country to
lay down their product in Liverpool at five pence
sterling per pound, *plus* freight and charges
(which is about the ante-war price), at a very
handsome profit in currency here. The currency
cost of production will increase somewhat, but
not materially.   Products of the soil will be affected less than anything else in the cost of production.   Thus, our cotton producers will be
enabled to regain their monopoly. I do not say
that it is good policy to exhaust our soil in sup-
plying Europe with food and raw materials; but
in the present condition of the country, political,
industrial, and financial, it will be advantageous

for a few years.[1] Other commodities, such as tobacco, and wheat, and corn, will be affected, as well as the wages of labor, but chiefly in consequence of the increased rapidity of the societary circulation, and to a very limited extent compared with cotton. The large advance in the currency price of cotton, as well as the advance in the currency price of foreign staples, such as tea, coffee, and sugar, will absorb so much currency in the circulation of those commodities, that the prices of other commodities cannot possibly advance materially. As a rule, it may be said that the average price of domestic commodities cannot possibly advance *pari passu* with the price of gold, unless the currency be increased, nor can they decline *pari passu* with the premium on gold, unless the currency be decreased. The wages of mechanical labor are, as a rule, about one hundred and fifty per cent. higher than before the war, while the price of gold is only forty per cent. higher. The volume of currency, *per capita*, is about two hundred per cent. greater than before the war, and if the societary circulation were rapid, the average price of commodi-

---

[1] If the instrument of association be adjusted, these things will regulate themselves. The economy of labor will become perfected.

ties and the average wages of labor would be two
hundred per cent. higher than before the war,
without regard to the premium on gold. The
average prices of commodities and the average
wages of labor cannot advance more than two
hundred per cent. above ante-war prices, unless
the *per capita* volume of the currency be increased more than two hundred per cent. above
the ante-war volume. Such commodities as are
chiefly exported, will advance the most in currency price, as the price of gold advances, and
such commodities as are not exported at all, will
advance the least. Rent will not be so much
affected, nor will the price of land. The eternal
law of supply and demand governs price. If
the currency value of the instrument of association be $1,500,000,000, so will be the average
currency prices, if the societary circulation be
healthy. If the gold value, or weight, of the
instrument of association be $500,000,000, so
will be the gold prices, if the societary circulation be healthy. Hence, the lower the gold
prices of commodities, the greater the exports
and the smaller the imports; and the higher the
gold prices of commodities, the greater the imports and the smaller the exports. Nothing can
be more favorable to the industry of the country,

and the credit of the government, than to permanently contract the gold value of the instrument of association to its *minimum.* Yet, strange as it may seem, the whole power of legislation, and the whole energy of the Treasury Department has been exerted to keep down the premium on gold, to expand the gold value of the instrument of association, to force excessive importation, to restrict exportation, to destroy the industry of the country, to imperil the credit of the government, to increase the burden of taxation, and to expel by hundreds of millions the interest bearing securities of the government. It cannot be denied that this empirical interference with the price of gold has been countenanced by public opinion, but the vagaries of public opinion on the subject of money, furnish a curious commentary on the philosophy of the human mind.[1] Precisely the opposite was the course that should have been pursued; the price of gold should have been maintained at its *maximum* point, but so infatuated is the public mind with the idea of the immense advantage to be derived from a low premium on gold, that those who entertain different views are regarded as fools; while the science of political economy seems to be held in unmeasured contempt. Nor

[1] Bowen.

will the currency prices of foreign commodities
advance *pari passu* with the premium on gold.
On the contrary, the gold prices of such foreign
commodities as can be produced in our own
country, especially manufactured articles, will be
forced below cost of production, and cease to be
imported, and the nation will become a large ex-
porter of manufactures. The currency prices of
articles of unnecessary and luxurious consumption will advance sufficiently high to check
consumption and importation thereof, to a very
considerable extent, thus exerting a salutary
influence on the habits of the people, which have
become corrupted by excessive exoticism. Coffee, tea, and sugar will, perhaps, advance in currency price more than any other commodities;
but their gold prices will remain at little more
than the cost of production, for the producing
countries, whence these commodities are imported, will be affected somewhat by the change
in the instrument of association. Absenteeism
will no longer cause such a heavy drain on our
resources, for absentees will find they can obtain
more for their money at home than abroad, and
will accordingly return. Smuggling will be
prevented to a great extent, for most commodities will be produced cheaper at home than

abroad, and therefore, smuggling will not pay. The art of ship-building will return from its voluntary exile, and the ringing blow of the axe will again reverberate throughout the land. American ships will no longer make their repairs and procure their outfits abroad ; on the contrary, foreign ships will, to a great extent, make repairs and procure outfits in the United States ; and if we do not regain our share of the carrying trade immediately, we shall be in a fair way of doing so very soon. Our public funds will no longer take wings and fly unto the uttermost parts of the earth, — sad evidences of maladministration, and of the abuse and neglect of the abundant resources vouchsafed to us by a beneficent God. The burden of taxation will no longer hang like a millstone on the necks of the people, eating up their capital, and sinking them deeper and deeper into the slough of bankruptcy. The present weight of the instrument of association, with gold at $1.40, is twice what it will be when it is adjusted : and it is this great weight which is breaking the people down ; this is the tax that must be removed, or society will fall back on its reserved rights — its natural rights that never lapse,[1] and repudiation of the public debt

[1] Gibbons.

will follow from necessity. Let not this danger
be regarded as improbable, for it is now impending; and if the current of events be not reversed,
it will surely come, and before a very long time
shall have passed. If repudiation does come, it
will not be the fault of the people, who have
borne taxation as no other people ever did before; but it will be the fault of those in the
executive and legislative departments of the government, who, intent only upon power and
gorged with the spoils of office, have manifested
neither the disposition nor capacity to manage
the affairs of state. Finally, the effect of this
adjustment upon the public credit, which is now
tottering, will be such as to render it secure beyond peradventure.

VI.

A PERFECT INSTRUMENT.

BEFORE discussing the essentials of a perfect instrument of association, it will be useful to examine into the character of that which was in use prior to the war. There are three sorts of currencies, from which it has been attempted, at various times, to form the instrument of association, here or in other countries. First, a pure currency, whose deposits are debt, and whose circulating moiety consists entirely of coin or coin certificates. Second, a mixed currency, whose deposits are debt, and whose circulating moiety is partly of coin, but mostly of promissory notes, supposed to be convertible into coin at the will and pleasure of the holder at all times. Third, an unmixed paper currency, whose deposits are debt, and whose circulating moiety is entirely of promissory notes inconvertible.[1] An instrument of association

---

[1] In a pure currency, the measure of value is comparatively fixed; in a mixed currency, it is constantly changing; in an unmixed paper currency, it is entirely abandoned.

formed from a pure currency, is an inestimable blessing, hitherto unknown to this country. An instrument of association formed from a mixed currency, is a chimera, a curse, an instrument of dissociation rather, a device of Satan to enthrone capital and enslave labor, and, insensibly and by slow degrees, to establish a moneyed aristocracy, disguised (if the disguise be not discarded in the course of time) under the form of democracy. An instrument of association formed from inconvertible paper, is a machine for creating civil war; for destroying both capital and labor, and for perpetuating military despotism as the alternative of anarchy. Before the war, the instrument of association was composed of a mixed currency—of circulating notes pretending to be convertible into specie on demand, and whose ultimate redemption was secured (?)[1] by state stocks bearing interest; and also of deposits, or inscribed credits on the books of the banks, which also pretended to be payable in coin on demand. These banks were banks of discount and deposit, and of issue, the last being an usurped function,[2] in order to perform which, the

[1] When the rebellion broke out, the circulation of those Western banks that was based on Southern stocks, became worthless. There can hardly be anything more absurd than to base a circulation upon debt. Debt upon debt.

[2] Bowen.

banks pretended to keep sufficient coin on hand
to be in a position to pay their bill-holders on
demand. They also pretended to retain coin
sufficient to meet all demand liabilities that were
likely to be called for, but they never did; the
whole system, from first to last, was a fraud.[1]
An inconvertible paper currency does not profess
anything, but this system professed everything;
it professed to be as good as gold, and cheaper:
it was neither; it was much more expensive.
The instrument of association thus formed was
never of uniform weight or measure.[2] Society
was pretty much in the same condition as if a
bushel of wheat were the standard of value, and
as if the bushel measure were sometimes shrunk
to a half bushel, and sometimes expanded to a
bushel and a half. Men incurring a debt to-day
on a basis of thirty pounds to a bushel, might,
through no fault of theirs, be suddenly called
upon to pay at the rate of ninety pounds to the
bushel.[3] The banks expanded this instrument
like a balloon, and then, with great suddenness,
pricked it, so that it would instantly collapse,
spreading ruin all about. Industry sometimes

---

[1] Walker. [2] *Ante*, pp. 58, 85.

[3] In 1837 the *per capita* was $17.60, and in 1843 it was
$6.18; in 1857 it was $15.60, and in 1858 it was $11.56.

7

would be rushing at fever heat, and at others, it
would be paralyzed, as if under the cold hand
of death.   I do not charge all this upon individuals or corporations,[1] but I charge it upon the
system.   The fatal defect of the system is that
the entire active currency [2] is debt, and is not
self-adjusting, because debt bearing no interest
cannot be exported.   The process of inflation is
initiated by an increase of loans and discounts,
and an increase of circulating notes; prices
begin to rise; speculators begin without capital, and buy merchandise, giving promissory
notes (on time) in payment; the payee gets
the notes discounted, thus increasing the deposits or wholesale currency; and wholesale
prices thus rising higher, retail prices respond,
which enables the banks to increase their circulating notes, or retail currency, and so the instrument is expanded without any increase of
value.[3]   Price only is gained.[4]   Imports then
begin to flow in, to be sold in a market where

---

[1] I have stated elsewhere that political economy assumes
nothing but the universality of human selfishness. Profit is
the motive of these inflations.

[2] Circulation and deposits.

[3] If the currency be a currency of value, it cannot be expanded without adding value.

[4] Walker. The increase of deposits may be preceded by
increase of circulation, but the increase in both is, necessarily,
nearly simultaneous.

the prices are high, and exports cease to flow out as usual, because prices are too high to show any profit abroad; and finally, coin begins to go, because coin or gold is the cheapest commodity we have to offer. Instead of purchasing wheat of us, England will take gold and purchase wheat in Russia. Now, if this currency were a currency of value, the coin would be taken directly from the active currency itself, thus reducing its weight, and prices would begin to fall; but the gold for export is not taken from the currency, and here is where the whole mischief lies; this is where the defect shows. If the currency were a pure currency, it could not be unduly inflated, because the export would reduce it as fast as it was increased. But the export is taken from the reserve of the banks, and not from the currency, therefore prices do not fall; on the contrary, they increase, for the movement has not spent its upward force, and the more they increase, the more gold is called for, till the banks get alarmed; and, having shrunk the measure of value, or lowered the standard, so that a half a bushel of wheat, or thirty pounds, is worth as much price as a whole bushel, or sixty pounds, was before the inflation, they are obliged to contract, because the founda-

tion of the superstructure is being rapidly under-
mined; for every dollar of coin taken from the
bank reserves, they are obliged to contract several
dollars of circulation and deposits,[1] panic ensues,
bill-holders run on the banks for specie, and the
depositors (as in 1857) threaten to draw their
deposits in coin, and the banks must suspend or
break; the final result being that the standard is
raised so that the banks can resume.   Then
those who have contracted debts on a basis of
thirty pounds to the bushel, are obliged to pay
on a basis of sixty pounds to the bushel, and the
result is failure and confiscation.   The whole
process of contraction under this mixed system
is precisely as if the walls of a brick building
that had been carried to an extreme elevation,
had to be reduced in height by undermining,
and taking out bricks from the foundation, thus
making a crash inevitable.   With a pure currency,
the elevation could never attain extreme height,
because the bricks would be taken off as fast as
they were put on.   This is why, under the
present system, the national banks could not
suffer any considerable contraction of legal
tenders; and this is one reason why the national
bank circulation should be displaced by legal

---

[1] Walker's chapters on mixed currency give an excellent
analysis of the subject.

tenders. Such is the character of the instrument of association, formed of a mixed currency, that was in use antecedent to the war. The inevitable consequence was disorganization of our whole social system. Manufacturing industry, that is to say, the products of labor alone, could not possibly compete with the products of labor of those countries where they had a currency less inflated. Our currency was constantly inflated; our channels of circulation were overflowing all the time. Hence our industry was diverted from manufacturing to agricultural pursuits; the products of the soil, and of our mines, were the only commodities that we could export to advantage. This state of things created an inordinate demand for the products of slave labor, and the system of slavery grew apace under this powerful material influence. Foreign nations were the largest consumers of the products of slave labor — the largest and best customers of the Slave States — and so the material interests of the Slave States were different from and opposed to those of the Free States. The Free States devoted themselves to manufacturing industry, partly on account of peculiarities of soil and of climate, and partly on account of the absence of slavery — of the presence

of a purer democracy, and a higher degree
of civilization.   It is difficult, perhaps, to dis-
tinguish the relation of cause and effect between manufacturing industry and a high civilization.   It is stated elsewhere that manufacturing industry is susceptible of the greatest
extension of the principle of the division of
labor,[1] and the greater the extent of the division
of labor in any community, the higher the civilization of such community.[2]   Be that as it may,
the Free States devoted themselves extensively to
manufacturing industry ; but manufacturing industry could not flourish as it ought, under such
a currency ; therefore recourse was had to protection.   A protective tariff was insisted upon
by the Manufacturing States of the North, not
for revenue especially, but avowedly for protecting manufactures that could not flourish under an
inflated currency.   The South objected to such a
tariff ; it vehemently denounced the "accursed
policy" of the tariff, if not justly, certainly nat-
urally, and perhaps with feelings akin to those
which actuated John Hampden.   He did not
oppose taxation because it would ruin his fortunes,
but because the principle upon which it was
levied made him a slave.[3]   The material interests

1 *Ante*, p. 16.
2 Everett, Guizot, Chenevix.   3 Burke.

of the South were wholly alienated from those of the North by a detestable currency. "What interest," asked Mr. Hayne, "has South Carolina in a canal in Ohio?" None whatever, from his point of view. The system of slavery was nurtured by a currency that was discouraging to manufactures and civilization, and favorable to the products of forced, unskilled labor, and to barbarism. And so alienation begat strife, and strife begat civil war. Slavery went down in the struggle, bequeathing a heavy debt and onerous taxation, and a currency with which our public men seem utterly incompetent to deal. Such is the result of violating the law of God in substituting a miserable paper currency — the immaterial shadow — in place of the real substance, which, so far as finite wisdom can comprehend the Infinite, was intended by the Creator to be the money of society — the instrument of association.[1] Credit is useful in its place. Mr. Webster never uttered a truer aphorism, perhaps, than when he said that the phrase "Those who trade on borrowed capital ought to break," was

1 "Thou shalt not have in thine house divers measures, a great and a small.

"But thou shalt have a perfect and just weight, a perfect and just measure shalt thou have; that thy days may be lengthened in the land which the Lord thy God giveth thee."— *Deut.* xxv. 14, 15.

the most aristocratic sentiment ever spoken in
this country.   Credit has its appropriate functions in the economy of society, but it never has
supported, and never will support a note circulation that will perform the functions of money
with any degree of satisfaction or security.
Value is the indispensable quality of money,
and the precious metals embody value in its
most convenient and economical form.   They
constitute the only proper material for the instrument of association ; and had it never been attempted to supersede a value currency in this
country by a debt currency, it is not too much
to say that there would have been no motive to
extend slavery, but a motive to extinguish it ;
there would have been no inducement to break
up the Union, but every incentive to knit the
fraternal bond more closely.   It is proper to say
that a demand for specie from this country may
arise from a sudden contraction of the circulation
and deposits of the Bank of England, in consequence of an export of coin from thence, or on
account of political troubles ; and in order to
strengthen the Bank of England, our banks
under the old system might at any time be
obliged to suspend.   It is a law of political
economy, that any considerable contraction of the

currency of any commercial country will cause
a flow of precious metals thither, precisely as air
will flow into and fill a vacuum.

Having said thus much of the instrument of
association as it existed anterior to the war, and
having analyzed the instrument of association as
it exists at present,[1] and having pointed out the
necessity and the method of adjusting the instrument,[2] it will be observed that the adjustment of
the existing instrument will, when it is effected,
leave us with a debt currency of circulation and
deposits, whose circulating moiety will consist
of notes of redemption, convertible into coin on
demand. The problem then presenting itself for
solution, is to substitute a metallic circulation in
place of the notes of redemption ; for it will be
observed, that although the notes of redemption
will be payable on demand, they will be, never-
theless, a note circulation, or, a circulation of
debt, and not a circulation of value. If the
present legal tender issue be not increased,[3] there
will be about $660,000,000 to be displaced by
the notes of redemption, at the rate of three for
one, making a circulation of the redemption notes
of about $220,000,000, an amount which is

---

[1] *Ante*, chap. ii.   [2] *Ante*, chaps. iii., iv.
[3] There is great danger of this.

quite as much as can be sustained at a convertible point.[1] It will be necessary to prohibit banks of issue in the United States, thus leaving the channels of circulation to be filled by the redemption notes alone. The withdrawal of the notes of redemption should be very gradual, not exceeding the value of our surplus gold product,[2] say at the rate of about fifty millions per annum, and in order to fill the vacuum created by the withdrawal of these notes,[3] the Secretary of the Treasury should be authorized and instructed by law to receive deposits of bullion, and grant certificates of deposit or receipts therefor, payable to bearer on demand, in sums of not less than $5,000.[4] He should also receive deposits of coin, and grant certificates of deposit or receipts therefor, payable to bearer on demand, in sums of not less than $5, nor more than $1,000; and such certificates of deposit, or receipts for bullion or coin, should be lettered and numbered so as

[1] This is a little more than $6 *per capita.* The currency in 1857 became inconvertible when the circulation was about $7 *per capita.*

[2] Beyond what may be needed for consumption in the arts.

[3] As these redemption notes are withdrawn, value will be needed to circulate other values, and the precious metals will begin to flow into the circulation.

[4] The object of these deposits of bullion is, that when there is an export drain, bullion will be taken instead of coin, thus saving the seigniorage.

to preserve the individuality of each certificate or receipt; and whenever any certificate or receipt, having been once issued, shall be presented and received into the Treasury for redemption, such certificate or receipt shall thereupon be canceled, and new certificates or receipts, with different letters and numbers, shall be issued against each new deposit of bullion or coin.[1] And whenever all the notes of redemption shall have been withdrawn, such certificates of deposit or receipts for bullion or coin, shall form the exclusive substitute[2] circulation of the country, the metallic circulation itself being used in sums under five dollars. It will be observed that the withdrawal of the notes of redemption will be a reduction of the debt, and the means to withdraw those notes must come from revenue. I have suggested fifty millions per annum as the amount to be withdrawn, because that is about our surplus gold product, and if the gold is not used for that purpose it will be sent abroad; but it cannot be exported except at a loss equal to the cost of transmission, and other products can be advantageously used instead, under a sound currency, in paying for our imports.[3] The revenue necessary

---

[1] This is intended as a check against forgery.

[2] That is to say, the substitute or proxy of the metal itself.

[3] If fifty millions per annum be thought excessive, a less

to retire this debt currency, could be derived from a tax on United States securities. I am aware that existing laws forbid the taxation of United States securities, and this restriction should remain in force as against state and municipal taxation. But the exemption of so large a portion of accumulated capital from taxation, and the imposition of the whole burden of taxation upon the wages of labor, rent, and profits, is subversive of public morals, calculated to cast odium upon the law, unendurable under a democratic form of government,[1] and menacing to the stability of the Union. Law is beneficence acting by rule.[2] Law is an instrument of justice, and whenever, from any cause, it becomes an engine of oppression, it will be more honored in the breach than the observance. Whenever the notes of redemption shall have been entirely withdrawn, the circulation will have become filled with the money of God and nature, and we shall have a pure currency, a perfect instrument of association. Labor will be no longer despoiled of its just rewards ; commerce may safely spread

sum could be applied for the purpose. The reasons for suggesting fifty millions are cogent.

[1] This exemption of capital from taxation is a violation of political economy, and contravenes the first of the four principles of taxation laid down by Adam Smith.

[2] Burke.

its wings to the perennial breeze; partisan warfare will cease its tumult,[1] and the country will have attained the happiest epoch in its history. Let it be forever understood that there shall be no banks of issue in the United States; let Congress fulfill its constitutional duty regarding the money of the country, and " regulate the value thereof;"[2] and then banks of deposit and discount may be established without limit, under wholesome regulations.

But here again, perhaps, the argument may be pressed upon us, that the notes of redemption, if not in excess, will remain convertible, and that it will be a great saving to use them, instead of the precious metals,[3] for the instrument of association. The answer to this is that the government, through its sub-treasury agencies, cannot exercise the functions of a bank of issue, and regulate the volume of these notes of redemption according to the changing pulse of commerce.[4]

---

[1] It is not expected that political divisions will cease, but party spirit will lose much of its malignity. Political rivalry will be a rivalry for good and not for evil; it will exercise salutary restraint upon the ascendant side.

[2] *Constitution*, art. 1, sec. 8, clause 5.

[3] *Ante*, p. 22.

[4] " It is not desirable that to the ever-growing attributions of the government, so delicate a function should be superadded."
— *Mill*.

The volume of notes will depend upon the condition of the public revenue and expense. Again, these notes are evidences of debt, and it is and has been the inevitable fate of such a currency, that, under some pretext or other, the issue is always increased to excess. The least deficit in the revenue, the least complaint of the burden of taxation will be the signal for increased issues. It must be conceded that the mass of the people, and the legislators of our country, are ignorant of the true principles of political economy, and especially of the theory of money. Nor do those who fill positions of trust in the executive departments of the government, seem to possess anything more than a superficial knowledge of this important subject. The deplorable ignorance of political economy manifested by our public men since the beginning of the war, has been most unfortunate in its results. And, especially, the management of the Treasury Department since the close of the war has been charlatanical and profligate in character. The history of the civilized world affords no parallel for such outrageous abuse of fiscal authority, and it is to be hoped that it never will. We have probably accumulated a foreign debt of eight hundred millions of dollars since the close of the war, which is entirely owing to mal-administration of this high trust. Congress must be held responsible for investing any minister of finance with such destructive power. The past and current history of the executive and legislative departments of our government is a warning to us not to trust any power over the currency to any man, or any body of men.[1] Such a power is seldom understood and always abused. The money of the country must be self-regulating, and if it be composed of value and not debt; if it be composed of the precious metals, though it bear the image and superscription of Cæsar; it is still the money of God, designed, doubtless, as one of the agents in preserving the harmony of the universe.

---

[1] The office of finance minister in this country, of late years, has commonly been occupied by what Adam Smith termed "that insidious and crafty animal, vulgarly called a statesman or politician, whose counsels are directed by the momentary fluctuation of affairs." Great national emergencies expose incompetent officials. It was so in England. Mr. Vansittart, who was Chancellor of the Exchequer from 1812 to 1822, "was simply a thoroughly incompetent mind;" and it was said by the opposition members of the House of Commons at that time, that "the present distresses were occasioned by having a miserable, miscalculating, puny Chancellor of the Exchequer, who did not know the resources of the country, owing to the ignorance and want of power of his little mind."

VII.

THE INSTRUMENT AS AFFECTED BY THE PRODUCT OF PRECIOUS METALS.

THE method of creating a perfect instrument of association has been shown, and it remains to demonstrate how this instrument can be maintained in all its perfection, notwithstanding that the surplus product of precious metals constantly tends to increase its weight and thus impair its efficiency; for it is a fundamental principle that the smaller the weight and value of the instrument, the greater its efficiency, and the greater the prosperity of the community.[1] By surplus product of precious metals, is meant that portion not needed for consumption in the arts, and which cannot remain in the country; for if it be attempted to increase the value and weight of the instrument, industry will languish, and beyond a certain weight the instrument will not be susceptible of further addition, and then the precious metals are expelled from the country as fast as produced. Supposing that 2,239,-

---

[1] *Ante*, p. 19.

583 pounds, troy weight, of standard gold, or
$500,000,000, is the *maximum* value and
weight of the instrument compatible with a
flourishing condition of society, it becomes manifest that the weight and value of this instrument
cannot be increased except at the expense of the
prosperity of the whole community.   It may be
increased, perhaps, twenty per cent., or possibly
more; but there is a limit beyond which it will
be impossible to increase it under any circumstances, and when this limit is reached, it will be
impossible to retain the surplus in the country.[1]
It might as well be attempted to stop the eternal
flow of waters over Niagara Falls.   Since it is
impossible to retain this surplus product of the
precious metals, and since the prosperity of the
country depends entirely upon the weight of
the instrument of association being maintained at
the lowest point permissible by the international
laws of trade, it is clearly the interest of the
people, that there be every possible, as well as
profitable inducement offered, for the exportation
of the entire surplus product of precious metals
as soon as produced.[2]   What inducement to ex-

---

[1] It is unnecessary to demonstrate this again.   Nothing is
more fully established in the science of political economy.

[2] Time is an important element in the economy of society.

8

port the precious metals may be offered without
detriment to the country at large, it is my purpose now to inquire. In doing this, I shall
touch upon a most interesting branch of the science of political economy, a branch which I
might well have wished to avoid, if it were possible, because it necessitates a survey of that
which has been the battle-ground of contending
parties since the formation of our separate
national existence. It is clear, from the foregoing, that so long as we continue to produce the
precious metals, the balance of account, or the
exchange, or, as it is called, the balance of trade,
will always be against us. But though the balance of trade may always be against us, the
balance of consumption, under proper legislation,
will always be in our favor.[1] It is obvious that
there can be no profit in exporting the precious
metals ; on the contrary, there will be a loss
equal to the cost of transmission ; but if the
precious metals can be used abroad to purchase
some commodity that will be reproductively con-

1 " There is another balance, indeed, which has already
been explained, very different from the balance of trade, and
which, according as it happens to be favorable or unfavorable,
necessarily occasions the prosperity or decay of every nation.
This is the balance of the annual produce and consumption."
— *Smith.*

sumed at home, such as wool, for instance, for less value than it will cost if produced at home, it is clear that the exchange will be to our advantage.[1] If, for instance, a dollar's worth of bullion exported will bring back three pounds of wool, of a quality equal to that which costs half a dollar per pound to produce at home, then it is clear, that while the balance of account, or balance of trade, will be against us, the balance of consumption will be largely in our favor. But if this bullion is exported at a loss, to purchase abroad that which is unproductively consumed at home, such as a finished silk fabric, whereon the science of production is ended, the balance of consumption is largely against us ; and in this case it were better that the bullion had been thrown into the sea,[2] rather than we should lose the cost of transmission abroad, and then again lose the unproductive-consumption-market[3]

---

[1] The exchange is profitable, not because we get more of human service or labor for a dollar than we could at home, but because we get more wool, which is not, except to a small extent, the product of human effort. Wealth is said to be the product of labor; more strictly speaking, it is the product of antecedent consumption, for labor itself is the product of previous consumption of food. Consumption and labor both may be unproductive, in which case poverty, and not wealth, is the result.

[2] Bowen.

[3] I mean by this, the home market for all commodities that

for commodities of home production ; for this
silk fabric, if consumed at home, interferes with
the product of home industry, and labor is the
only source of wealth.   Price is no criterion of
the advantage or disadvantage of commerce.
The money balance for or against us is no
evidence of a favorable foreign trade, or otherwise.   In the case we have supposed, the
labor of those who extracted the bullion from
the mines and brought it to the seaboard was
thrown away.   " The balance of consumption,"
says Adam Smith, " may be constantly in favor
of a nation, though what is called the balance
of trade may be generally against it." [1]   This
was the case where we supposed the wool was
received in exchange for the bullion.   And, on
the other hand, where the finished silk fabric
was received in exchange for the bullion, both
the balance of trade and balance of consumption were against us.   In the cases which we
have supposed, the so-called free trader contends
that it is advantageous to import that which
is unproductively consumed (the finished silk
fabric), if it can be imported for less money than
it will cost if produced at home.   And the so-

are unproductively consumed.   " The division of labor is limited by the extent of the market." — *Smith.*

[1] This principle seems to be entirely ignored by modern
writers who advocate what is called free trade.

called protectionist would prohibit that which is reproductively consumed (the raw wool), if it can be produced at home, and so protect home industry. Both ignore the balance of consumption ; both are wrong ;[1] both may be honest in their views. " Of all these false theories," says Mill, " the most notable is the doctrine of Protection to Native Industry ; a phrase meaning the prohibition, or the discouragement

[1] The protectionist forgets that wool is chiefly the creation of Omnipotence, and that it is reproductively consumed. The value added to the wool when it has become a finished textile, is entirely the work of man, and this finished textile is unproductively consumed. So far as that parcel of wool is concerned, the science of production is ended. The labor employed in making up the materials is the same, whether using foreign or domestic goods.

If the money value of commodities exchanged were the criterion of the advantageousness of foreign trade, I am quite satisfied that the protectionist of the present Congressional school occupies an untenable position. As it is, duties upon raw wool, or any other commodity of reproductive consumption, are wholly indefensible upon any principle of political economy; they necessarily work injury to the material prosperity of the country; they favor foreign industry and are inimical to home industry. I can conceive of no possible circumstances justifying such a violation of economical law. The greater the fiscal embarrassments of a nation, the stronger the argument for the free admission of all commodities reproductively consumed. Reproductive consumption is wealth itself, and should be encouraged, especially since the " balance of trade " must be against us so long as we produce a surplus of the precious metals. If we cannot preserve a favorable balance of trade, we must preserve a favorable balance of consumption.

by heavy duties, of such foreign commodities as
are capable of being produced at home." This
is a perfectly fair statement of the doctrine of
protection as exemplified by Congress, but it is
not the doctrine of protection as sanctioned by
the laws of political economy. It is the attempt
to get rich by legislation; it is the everlasting
search after the philosopher's stone. The true
doctrine of protection may be stated thus: the
discouragement, by heavy duties, of such foreign
commodities as are unproductively consumed,
and the encouragement, by free admission, of
such foreign commodities as are reproductively
consumed. Unproductive consumption of domestic commodities is the consumption of that
which had previously been produced within the
nation; and so far as the wealth of the nation is
concerned, the effect thereof is negative.[1] I am
not speaking of the consumption of matter, for
that is created by God; but I am speaking of
the consumption of utility — that " unsubstantial, intangible, abstract commodity, composed of
time, intellect, and exertion,"[2] commonly known
as labor, utility, or value, which is all that man

---

[1] If unproductive consumption exceeds production, wealth
decreases. If it equals production, wealth is neither increased
nor decreased. If it be less, wealth accumulates.

[2] Chenevix.

produces. Unproductive consumption of foreign commodities that were not produced within the nation, on the other hand, is a net loss. In the first instance, the nation gains by production and loses by consumption. In the latter instance, the nation loses by consumption but had not previously gained by production. The modern free trader says this is of no consequence, for the whole world is one community, and what America loses some other nation gains, and so it is the very best thing that could happen. The partisans of the two opposing doctrines are thus spoken of by Say: " The merchants and manufacturers, who seldom look beyond the actual sale of their products, or inquire into the causes which may operate to extend their sale, have warmly supported a position apparently so consistent with their interests; the poets, who are ever apt to be seduced by appearances, and do not consider themselves to be wiser than politicians and men of business, have been loud in the praise of luxury; and the rich have not been backward in adopting principles that exalt their ostentation into a virtue, and their self-gratification into benevolence." The motto, free trade, expresses an abstract, impracticable, Utopian idea. No commercial nation, civilized or uncivil-

ized, practices free trade ; nor is it possible that
they should, for free trade is incompatible with
national existence.[1]   International free trade is
destructive of national free trade.   There is a
vast field for philanthropic enterprise at home,
within the jurisdiction of our own laws, where rail-
road, telegraph, and other monopolies flourish.
But when other nations preach to us the human-
izing, Christianizing, liberalizing, civilizing doctrines of free trade, is it too much to ask them to
practice at home what they preach abroad ? And,
on the other hand, the doctrine of protection, as
it is too commonly understood among us, seems to
be nothing more than an attempt to counteract the
effects of a redundant currency, and to get rich by
excessive duties on foreign commodities.   The advocates of this kind of protection seem to forget
that the prices of commodities in this, or any country, depend upon the condition of the currency, and
upon the law of supply and demand. The principle
of protection within its proper limits is undoubt-
edly sound, and it is the sacred duty of every
government to extend the shield of its protection,
so far as may be needful, over every laudable

---

[1] " To expect, indeed, that the freedom of trade should
ever be entirely restored in Great Britain, is as absurd as to
expect that an Oceana or Utopia should ever be established
in it." — *Smith.*

enterprise of its people; but the first step towards protection is the establishment of a sound currency. This theory of spontaneity, however; this idea that industry and the various arts will spring into existence without careful culture and solicitation, is unfounded in political economy or common sense. We might as well expect fields of wheat and corn to spring into existence without the aid of the physical and mental powers of man.[1] In this exceedingly practical age, when the jealousies of trade are sharp and unscrupulous, it is criminal for any government to hold itself neutral in the contest, not caring whether those from whom it derives its support by heavy taxation, sink or swim under the weight of their accumulated burdens. " Strictly speaking," says Say, "there is no act of government but what has some influence on production." A government, therefore, cannot be neutral in such a contest; it must aid in striking down its own people's industries, or it must extend its helping hand to hold them up. Adam Smith himself admits that the establishment of any new manufacture, or branch of commerce, or new practice in agriculture, is always a speculation, and the losses contingent thereupon are com-

[1] Phillips.

monly greater than the profits; but when the
new enterprise becomes well known, the competition reduces the profits to the level of other trades.
But the free trader will say, that the artisan who
employs his time in making a finished silk fabric
with the aid of machinery can be more profitably
employed at some other pursuit, if the silk fabric
can be imported for less money than it will cost
when produced at home.[1] The answer to this is,
that so far as the nation is concerned, no amount
of reasoning can show it to be advantageous to
import that which is unproductively consumed,
no matter what the price may be. Price is not
alone to be considered. The character of the
consumption is the criterion. If the consumption of any imported article be productive, or reproductive, it increases the wealth of the nation.
If it be unproductive, it destroys the wealth of
the nation. Manufacturing industry is susceptible
of the most extended application of the principle
of the division of labor, and therefore manufacturing industry is most profitable and most civilizing[2] to the nation. Nothing can compensate a
nation for diverting its industry from the mechan-

---

[1] His labor cannot possibly be so productive, either to himself or his country, in any other pursuit than that for which
he is especially adapted by habit and natural gift.

[2] *Ante*, pp. 16, 102.

ical arts, provided that form of industry be not
excessively cultivated, to the exclusion of agriculture.[1] Mechanical industry is preëminently
the conquest of mind over matter,[2] and whenever
that form of industry is assailed, the revenue of
the state suffers, and its civilization is impaired.
But the free trader says, to restrict the importation of foreign manufactures, is to destroy foreign
commerce. Supposing this were so, is foreign
commerce the *summum bonum* of our existence ?
But it is not so. "The increase of domestic
industry lays the foundation of foreign commerce."[3] To what is the vast and profitable
foreign commerce of England owing, except it
be to the enormous development of her manufacturing industry ? A form of industry, the
vast extent of which was called into being by
the most unscrupulous and tyrannical commercial
policy that has yet disgraced the annals of history.
A policy which Adam Smith characterized as
a " manifest violation of the most sacred rights
of mankind." It need not be wondered at
that Adam Smith was a free trader, living, as he
did, at a time when such atrocious legislation

---

[1] This is the great economical mistake of England.

[2] A. von Humboldt.

[3] Hume. "Manufactures are, in almost all countries, the
chief support of foreign trade." — *Smith.*

was resorted to, for the purpose of establishing a manufacturing monopoly, against which no competition was allowed to lift its head, — a monopoly which it is now sought to perpetuate, under pretensions of liberality.[1] If, then, it be disadvantageous to the nation at large to import the finished silk fabric, how does it affect the artisan himself, whose occupation is thus cruelly destroyed ? He can become a scavenger, perhaps ; but the ranks of that useful class of people are already full, and if he adds himself to that class, it will tend to break down the wages of the whole. He can become a farm laborer, perhaps ; but there is already a surplus of labor in that direction, so much so, that corn has been used for fuel in the Western portion of our country. He has no capital but his industry. "He does not choose to expatriate himself. His whole capital, like himself, is American. He is rooted in the soil. He is not a cosmopolite as to industry and arts ; he is an American." [2] The pursuit of

---

[1] England gives free admission to cotton, because it is reproductively consumed ; she lays a heavy impost upon raw tobacco, which is unproductively consumed; and a still heavier impost upon manufactured tobacco, which is even more un-productively consumed. (Tariff of 1859.) This is sound economical policy, but a policy which only by a gross abuse of language can be denominated free trade. It is a policy precisely that for which I contend. It is protection.

[2] Phillips.

happiness is declared to be one of the unalien-
able rights of man, with which he has been
endowed by his Creator; and it is no less a
crime against God than an outrage upon the
artisan, to rob him of his capital, and condemn
him, and those whom God has given him, to the
pursuit of wretchedness.   No! there is no
nobler, no more sacred duty of a government,
than that which imposes upon it the necessity of
protecting the industry of a patriotic people, who
hold everything that is most dear to them at the
call of their country.   But the most efficacious,
and the only method of protecting the industry
of the people, is to perfect the instrument of
association, and to maintain it in perfection by
encouraging the export of the surplus product
of precious metals.   In order to encourage the
export of precious metals, it will be necessary to
encourage the import of all commodities that
are productively or reproductively consumed, and
to discourage the import of all commodities that
are unproductively consumed.   This is the only
principle involved in tariff legislation.   There
can be no greater blow to industry than to
maintain the instrument of association at an excessive value, or weight.   It is most singular
that the protectionist mind has generally favored

an enlarged currency.[1]   A recent convention of
manufacturers favored the maintenance and extension of the national bank system;[2] while a
leading metropolitan journal, devoted to the
interests of protection, advocated the immediate
resumption of specie payments, without any
preceding contraction of the currency, but
rather with an expansion, if anything, as a
means to protect home industry, — a measure,
than which, nothing could be more fatal to the
industry of the country, if it were possible.   A
pestilence which should sweep off every mechanic
and artisan in the country, could scarcely be
more fatal.   Our export trade would be brought
to a halt, and our import trade would be immensely increased, till the people were rapidly
exhausted, as they are now being exhausted.
Yet such is the fatuity of the popular mind upon
this subject.   It seems a paradox to the unreflecting mind, but it is true, that the lower the
premium on gold, the greater the depreciation of
the currency, and *vice versa.   As money increases
in quantity it declines in value, and as it declines
in quantity it increases in value.*   This is an

---

[1] Mr. Carey seems to be no exception to the rule. Professor
Bowen, however, is clear upon the subject.

[2] Cleveland, May 27, 1868.

axiom.[1] If, therefore, our currency (circulation and deposits) is $1,400,000,000 nominally, then, with gold at $1.40, the quantity of this currency is $1,000,000,000; with gold at $2.00, the quantity is $700,000,000. Hence, as the premium on gold advances, the currency depreciates in quantity and appreciates in value; and (reversing the language but retaining the sense of the axiom laid down by Smith) as the exchange is always in *favor* of that nation which maintains an *appreciated* currency, imports decrease, and exports increase. Our public men seem too obtuse to perceive this pregnant truth.[2]

The instrument of association is constantly in danger of being injuriously affected by the product of precious metals, and if the instrument of association is impaired, agriculture, manufactures, and commerce decline; civilization is retarded, and internecine strife is sure to follow, with stronger reason, now that there is a heavy burden of taxation to be borne. Therefore, the surplus product[3] of precious metals should be exported

---

[1] *Ante*, p. 63.

[2] The agio of the currency is one thing, and its depreciation quite another and very different. The depreciation is inversely as the agio. The public mind is confused on this point.

[3] It is hardly necessary to say that by surplus product is meant that portion for which there is no profitable use in the country.

as soon as produced, and every economical
means should be employed to facilitate that laudable purpose, taking care that we receive an
equivalent in exchange, so as to preserve the
balance of consumption in our favor.   If our
bonds can be bought back, thus canceling our
interest bearing debt to foreign nations, it will be
a beneficent result.   The tariff legislation, therefore, should be framed to preserve the instrument
of association unimpaired, and to provide revenue.   To this end, all commodities of reproductive consumption, such as raw materials, raw
produce, the constituents of paper, unmanufac-
tured metals, chemicals, and dye-stuffs, should be
admitted free.   All commodities of productive
consumption should be taxed at the *maximum*
revenue rate; that is to say, the duties should
not be so high as to check consumption nor
afford very great inducement to smugglers to
pursue their nefarious traffic.   The alimentary
substances, such as tea, coffee, and sugar,[1] chiefly
come into this category, and I judge that
\$65,000,000 per annum can be realized from
these three commodities.   If industry be well
employed, such a scale of duties would not
operate to check consumption.   All commodities

---

[1] Drugs and medicines, so far as they produce health, are
productively consumed.

of unproductive consumption, such as finished textiles, manufactures of all kinds in their last stage of completion, wines and spirits, tobacco, cosmetics, *bijouterie*, and all articles of luxurious consumption, should be subjected to such a scale of duties as would tend to prohibit and discourage consumption thereof. It is no hardship to lay a heavy impost upon luxuries, and other commodities unproductively consumed. The payment of such taxes is entirely within the option of the people; if any person pays such a tax, it is because he voluntarily subjects himself to it. The commodity is not essential to his comfort nor included among his necessities; rather the reverse. Such taxes do not necessarily fall upon the wages of labor, rent, or profits; they differ from all other taxes, in that they fall upon and are paid by the consumers without any retribution.[1] They are especially just and politic, because the consumption of such commodities of foreign production is hostile to the public interest.[2] With such tariff legislation, the instrument of association would remain perfect, and home industry be amply protected.

[1] Smith.
[2] " And is in every respect hurtful to the society." — Ibid.

I have not thought it proper, in this volume, to discuss the terms upon which the public debt can be funded into bonds, terminable only by redemption, at the pleasure of the government. I have merely to suggest that the burden of taxation should be made as light as possible; that the people hereafter shall have no reason to complain of injustice. So long as the material interests of the people are subserved by the maintenance of the Union, so long will the Union endure. If the instrument of association be perfect, and the burden of taxation be not excessive, we may reasonably expect it to endure for centuries. But if the true principles of political economy and political philosophy are contemned, there are those living who will see it shattered into fragments.[1]

[1] "Abstract liberty," said Burke, "is not to be found. Liberty inheres in some sensible objects. . . . The great contests for freedom in this country (England) were from the earliest times chiefly upon the question of taxing. . . . On this point of taxes. the ablest pens and most eloquent tongues have been exercised; the greatest spirits have acted and suffered. . . . The colonies draw from you, as with their life-blood, these ideas and principles. Their love of liberty, as with you, fixed and attached on this specific point of taxing. Liberty might be safe or might be endangered in twenty other particulars without their being much pleased or alarmed. Here they felt its pulse; and as they found that beat, they thought themselves sick or sound."

"Taxes," as Adam Smith truly remarks, "are badges of liberty;" but it is essential that they should be levied for just, laudable, and necessary purposes.   When levied for other objects they become badges of slavery, and whatever laws Congress may have passed, or shall hereafter pass, "nobody will be argued into slavery."

"Est igitur respublica res populi; populus autem non omnis hominum cœtus, quoque modo congregatus, sed cœtus multitudinis juris consensu et utilitatis communione sociatus." — *Cicero.*